Admiring and Applauding God

Admiring and Applauding God

Meditations on the Excellencies of God's Character

R. BRUCE STEVENS
Foreword by Darrell Bustin

RESOURCE *Publications* · Eugene, Oregon

ADMIRING AND APPLAUDING GOD
Meditations on the Excellencies of God's Character

Copyright © 2015 by R. Bruce Stevens. All rights reserved. Except for brief quotations in critical publications or reviews, no part of this book may be reproduced in any manner without prior written permission from the publisher. Write: Permissions, Wipf and Stock Publishers, 199 W. 8th Ave., Suite 3, Eugene, OR 97401.

Resource Publications
An Imprint of Wipf and Stock Publishers
199 W. 8th Ave., Suite 3
Eugene, OR 97401

www.wipfandstock.com

ISBN 13: 978-1-4982-0144-5

Manufactured in the U.S.A.   03/19/2015

Dedicated to

Edmund Reuel Hutchins,

our cherished little friend of God,

who now enjoys the rich protection

of his heavenly Father

Contents

Begin the Day with God | xiii
Foreword by Darrell Bustin | xv
Introduction | xvii
How to Use This Book | xix

Ability-giver | 1
Acceptor | 2
Adopter | 3
Afflicter | 4
Alien-lover | 5
Anger-restrainer | 6
Angry One | 7
Animal-lover | 8
Anointer | 9
Approachable One | 10
Arm-strengthener | 11
Arouser of the Wicked | 12
Attitude-changer | 13
Author | 14
Avenger | 15
Awesome | 16
Beautiful | 17
Bestower of Favors | 18
Binder | 19
Binder | 20
Bird-knower | 21
Blesser | 22
Boldness-giver | 23
Bread | 24
Brother | 25

Burden-bearer | 26
Caller | 27
Carrier | 28
Celebrator | 29
Changeless | 30
Chastener | 31
Chariot-owner | 32
Chooser | 33
City-watcher | 34
Cloud-rider | 35
Comforter | 36
Commander of Angels | 37
Commander of Nature | 38
Companion | 39
Compassionate | 40
Confidence | 41
Confronter | 42
Consoler | 43
Cord-cutter | 44
Counselor | 45
Covenant-maker | 46
Covenant-rememberer | 47
Coverer | 48
Craftsman | 49
Creator | 50

Cross-bearer | 51
Crowner | 52
Curdler | 53
Curse-bearer | 54
Defender of Widows | 55
Delighter | 56
Deliverer from Graves | 57
Deliverer | 58
Demon-caster | 59
Demon-master | 60
Desire-giver | 61
Destroyer | 62
Director | 63
Discernment-giver | 64
Disciplinarian | 65
Disgrace-remover | 66
Dismantler | 67
Displayer of His Holiness | 68
Doer of the Immeasurable | 70
Door-opener | 71
Dragger | 72
Drawer | 73
Ear-turner | 74
Enabler | 75
Encourager | 76
Endurance-giver | 77
Enemy-lover | 78
Engraver | 79
Enricher | 80
Enthroned One | 81
Eternal | 82
Ever-present One | 83
Examiner | 84
Executioner | 85
Exerciser | 86
Eye-opener | 87
Eye-ranger | 88
Eye-turner | 89

Face-shiner | 90
Faithful One | 91
Faith-giver | 92
Famine-sender | 93
Father | 94
Father to the Fatherless | 95
Feeder | 96
Fever-lifter | 97
Fighter | 98
Fire | 99
Fire-master | 100
Food-provider | 101
Foot-setter | 102
Foot-steadier | 103
Footstep-director | 104
Foot-washer | 105
Forgiver | 106
Fortress | 107
Fragrance-spreader | 108
Freedom-giver | 109
Friend | 110
Fruit-grower | 111
Frustrater of the Wicked | 112
Gate | 113
Gift | 114
Gift-giver | 115
Giver of Eternal Life | 116
Giver of Undivided Hearts | 117
Giver-overer | 118
Glorious Name | 119
God of Gods | 120
Grace-abounder | 121
Gracious | 122
Grandchild-blesser | 123
Griever | 124
Guardian | 125
Guide | 126
Hair-counter | 127

Hand-holder | 128
Hand-placer | 129
Head-lifter | 130
Heart-changer | 131
Heart-former | 132
Heart-hardener | 133
Heart-holder | 134
Heart-looker | 135
Heart-mover | 136
Heart-opener | 137
Heart-toucher | 138
Heart-turner and Director | 139
Helper | 140
Hemmer | 142
Holy | 143
Home-blesser | 144
Honorer | 145
Hope-giver | 146
House-builder | 147
Humbler | 148
Hurler | 149
Husband | 150
Impartial | 151
Jealous | 152
Joy | 153
Joyful | 154
Joy-giver | 155
Judge | 156
Just | 157
Justice-granter | 158
Justice-lover | 159
Justifier | 160
Keeper | 161
Key-holder | 162
Killer | 163
King | 164
King-crusher | 165
Knitter | 166

Lamb of God | 167
Lamp | 168
Lamp-bearer | 169
Law-abolisher | 170
Leader | 171
Leaver | 172
Life | 173
Life-giver | 174
Life-holder | 175
Life Preserver | 176
Lifter | 177
Light of the World | 178
Light-wrapper | 179
Longing God | 180
Looker on the Lowly | 181
Lopper | 182
Lord | 183
Lord of Lords | 184
Love-abounder | 185
Lover | 186
Majestic | 187
Maker of Heaven and Earth | 188
Maker of People | 189
Mediator | 190
Memorial-giver | 191
Merciful | 193
Messiah | 194
Mighty | 195
Mildew-spreader | 196
Mind-reader | 197
Mocker | 198
Moth | 199
Mountain-treader | 200
Nation-healer | 201
Nation-judger | 202
Nation-watcher | 203
Orphan-defender | 204
Overcomer | 205

Owner | 206
Panic-sender | 207
Path-maker | 208
Path-straightener | 209
Peace | 210
Peace-giver | 211
Peacekeeper | 212
Piercer of Darkness | 213
Pity-causer | 214
Planner | 215
Plan-placer | 216
Portion-assigner | 217
Potter | 218
Preserver | 219
Procession-leader | 220
Promise-keeper | 221
Promise-maker | 222
Promise-rememberer | 223
Protector | 224
Provider | 225
Quickener | 226
Quieter | 227
Raiser | 228
Rampart | 229
Ransom | 230
Rebuker | 231
Reconciler | 232
Redeemer | 233
Refiner | 234
Refuge | 235
Repayer | 236
Rescuer | 237
Rest-giver | 238
Restorer | 239
Revealer | 240
Rewarder | 241
Rich | 242
Righteous | 243

Rock | 244
Ruler | 245
Sabbath-master | 246
Satisfier | 247
Savior | 248
Searcher | 249
Seed-supplier | 250
Seeker | 251
Sender | 252
Servant | 253
Setter | 254
Shepherd | 255
Shield | 256
Sin-exposer | 258
Singer | 259
Sin-remover | 260
Sin-restrainer | 261
Sin-treader | 262
Sleep-granter | 263
Song | 264
Sparrow-rememberer | 265
Spirit-sender | 266
Stooper | 267
Strengthener | 268
Striker | 269
Strong | 270
Stronghold | 271
Sustainer | 272
Sweeper and Turner | 273
Sword | 274
Task-assigner | 275
Teacher | 276
Tester | 277
Thinker | 278
Thirst-quencher | 279
Thorn-giver | 280
Thought-evaluator | 281
Thunderer | 282

Tower | 283
Trainer | 284
Tree | 285
Troubler of Nations | 286
Truth | 287
Unchanging | 288
Understanding-giver | 289
Unfailing Lover | 290
Unity-giver | 291
Upholder | 292
Victory-giver | 293

Vine | 294
Waiter | 295
Watcher | 296
Whistler | 297
Wisdom-giver | 298
Wise | 299
Womb-opener | 300
Worker | 301
Wounder | 302
Wrath | 304
Yoke-giver | 305

Begin the Day with God

Every morning lean thine arms awhile
Upon the window-sill of heaven
And gaze upon the Lord,
Then, with the vision in thy heart,
Turn strong to meet the day.
—Thomas Blake

Foreword

"Look at that!"

Who can ever resist responding to those words? It seems no matter what else we are doing at the time, whenever we hear those words, we can't help but turn our eyes toward the object of attention.

In his book, *Admiring and Applauding God*, Bruce is basically saying to us, "Look at that!" It is so easy to rush past verses without stopping to truly look at what they are saying—especially verses which are familiar to us. In the following pages, over and over again, Bruce says, "Look at that! Look at the amazing view of God that we find in this verse." The descriptions will fire your imagination!

Some will sound impressive—*Awesome, Refuge, Protector*.

Some will sound well-known—*Shepherd, Light of the World, Creator*.

Some will sound puzzling—*Fire-master, Panic-sender, Light-wrapper*.

Some will sound politically correct—*Orphan-defender, Counselor, Animal-lover*.

Some will sound so downright curious that we will be tempted to jump ahead to read them—*Moth, Lopper, Stooper*.

(Be honest, have you ever thought of God as a Curdler?)

But these 300 pictures of the Person of God are not designed to entertain us. Each one is chosen to help us see the Lord just a little more clearly so that we will adore him more deeply. It's that simple. The images are drawn straight from the Bible. The insights Bruce gives are straightforward and uncluttered.

I have known Bruce for many years. He was one of my early mentors during my time at seminary. I sincerely appreciated him then, and that appreciation has only grown deeper over the years. As I learned the ropes of ministry serving alongside him, several aspects of his character were consistently evident. He was approachable, thirsty for God, lovingly truthful, all with a life marked by integrity. Not surprisingly, those same words come to mind as I read these pages.

Foreword

One of the things I love about this book is that it didn't start as a tool for teaching others. Bruce began collecting these thoughts as a learner. It was born out of a personal desire to become better at adoring his Lord and Savior. It was only later that God planted the idea in his heart that there were others who had similar struggles in focusing on his character, who could benefit from these glimpses into God's extraordinary nature. And thus this book was born.

If you are like me, you will be grateful for this book, in which Bruce taps us on the shoulder to get our attention and then points to a verse and says with wonder, "Look at that!"

Darrell Bustin

Introduction

I was taught early on that when it comes to prayer, there are four basic components: Adoration, Confession, Thanksgiving, and Supplication, known by the acronym ACTS. Eventually I found it more helpful to revise this handy framework into terms easier for me to identify with—PCAT, for Praise, Confession, Asking, and Thanksgiving.

I found that of these four parts of prayer, I could easily spend time in three. I was aware of both my own sinfulness and blessedness, so Confession and Thanksgiving were easy. And of course, who struggles with the Asking part of prayer? But Praise—now, that was a different matter. It was not for lack of desire that I struggled to praise God in prayer. I wanted to praise him as the Psalmist instructs, "Praise the Lord, O my soul; all my inmost being, praise his holy name" (Ps 103:1), but I just could not think of a way to consistently do so when I prayed. I sense many Christians struggle in much the same way.

I also found that I struggled to keep clear in my mind the distinction between thanking God and praising him. What I found helpful was this: Thanksgiving in prayer focuses on what God has done for me or has given to me, while Praise focuses on the person of God himself—what kind of person he is. Perhaps an example would be helpful. God is a Planner. Praising God as a Planner would focus on his amazing ability to make and implement plans for the world, nations, families, and individual people. Whereas we struggle to make plans for one day, even for one person, much less to successfully carry them out, God effortlessly makes plans for billions of people and carries out these plans flawlessly. How amazing is he to do that! Thanksgiving would focus on thanking God for his plans—past, present and future, including the plan of salvation, the plan to bring all things under the Lordship of Christ, and the plans he has for us and our loved ones.

I believe that God, in response to my desire to learn how to better praise and adore him, gave me an immensely practical insight to help me

Introduction

when I pray. It is my hope that what has proven helpful for me will aid my readers as well.

For several years during my devotional time, I had been noting the Bible passages that gave insight into the person and working of God. When it first happened, it was as if a light bulb went off. I began to see praiseworthy aspects of God's character and nature everywhere. These insights enabled me to focus on his greatness and goodness, leading me to naturally delight in him and spend time complimenting him on his admirable qualities. Most of the words I found were verbs, which I then converted into nouns. Some of the terms I came up with may cause grammarians to cringe a bit; nevertheless, I believe the form is helpful in conveying certain aspects of God's nature.

The verses I use are from the 1984 edition of the New International Version (NIV). If you use the NIV, you might find that your version may have some slightly different phrasing due to revisions to the NIV since it was first published.

How to Use This Book

A suggested method for using this book is to select one of the terms as the beginning point of your prayer time and then reflect on the verse, the term, and what it reveals of God. Take time to let your mind run with the term, meditating and reflecting on its meaning and then applying that meaning to God to reveal something of his nature. The Holy Spirit will likely bring to your mind additional thoughts (or thoughts more helpful to your life circumstances) related to the term than those I include. The few descriptions I have provided will hopefully provoke your own thinking and application.

Following a time of praising God, it is natural to drift into giving thanks, confessing, and asking God to help us and those we love in the very area upon which we have been meditating.

Ability-giver

But remember the Lord your God, for it is he who *gives you the ability* to produce wealth, and so confirms his covenant, which he swore to your forefathers, as it is today.

—Deut 8:18

- We owe our abilities in life to a variety of sources, e.g., our parents, teachers, professors, etc., and from our own study and life experiences.
- God is an Ability-giver. As the Israelites were poised to enter the promised land, they were warned not to forget the Lord or mistakenly think they had attained that land or prospered in it due to their own abilities. We face a similar temptation, forgetting that "Every good and perfect gift is from above, coming down from the Father of the heavenly lights, who does not change like shifting shadows" (Jas 1:17). God gives us our parents, our unique genetic code, our health, our temperament, and opportunities to go to school, get a job, and more. Our possessions and accomplishments have very little to do with us but everything to do with God. If we were born in another time or place, our lives would be so different. What we have in life and what we have attained in life ultimately comes from God.
- Praise God, our Ability-giver.

Acceptor

Then Peter began to speak: "I now realize how true it is that God does not show favoritism but *accepts men* from every nation who fear him and do what is right."

—Acts 10:34–35

- It is upsetting when qualified people are bypassed by hiring managers because a less-qualified relative or family friend was hired instead.
- We tend to exclude others who are not like us or who do not share our race, denomination, theology, social standing, politics, etc. We consciously and unconsciously judge who is worthy of our acceptance.
- God does not show favoritism but is willing to accept people regardless of their past sins, their family status, their education, appearance, etc.
- Jesus is the reason we have been accepted by God the Father, despite the fact that we had ignored or rejected him for years.
- Praise the Lord, who accepts us when we had no merit of our own.
- Praise God, who invites any and all to come to him and find acceptance.

Adopter

For he chose us in him before the creation of the world to be holy and blameless in his sight. In love *he predestined us to be adopted as his sons* through Jesus Christ, in accordance with his pleasure and will . . .

—Eph 1:4–5

- Adoption is a wonderful practice. Children who have no parents to love them—orphans, wards of the state, and street children—are welcomed into the hearts and homes of loving families.
- Praise God, who loved us enough to adopt us into his family, not caring about our past.
- Praise God that Jesus is willing to consider us his brothers and sisters: "So Jesus is not ashamed to call them brothers" (Heb 2:11b). And, "He replied, 'My mother and brothers are those who hear God's word and put it into practice'" (Luke 8:21).

Afflicter

I know, O Lord, that your laws are righteous,
and in faithfulness *you have afflicted me.*

—Ps 119:75

"Before I was *afflicted* I went astray, but now I obey your word"

—Ps 119:67

"It was good for me to be *afflicted* so that I might learn you decrees"

—Ps 119:71

- Most of our notions about affliction are entirely negative—we picture leprosy, cancer, and worse. But affliction can be a good thing. It can motivate us to change our direction, attitudes, or behavior.
- God loves us enough to use the hard side of love—to do whatever is necessary for us to be safe and to teach us to be better people.
- Praise God for his wise, fatherly love, even when it is expressed in affliction.
- Reflect on Jesus, who chose to be afflicted so that we could experience the love and forgiveness of God the Father.

Alien-lover

He defends the cause of the fatherless and the widow, and *loves the alien*, giving him food and clothing.

—Deut 10:18

- When the Bible speaks of aliens, it does not refer to little green men in spaceships. Rather, it refers to those who have left their birth country to live in a foreign land. Many aliens live as second-class citizens and do not enjoy the privileges or blessings of native citizens.
- God loves aliens. God's plan from the early pages of the Bible was to bless all nations and peoples through Abraham and Israel so that all would enjoy full citizenship in God's kingdom, regardless of their nation of birth.
- Praise the Lord for his love for the defenseless and the weak—the alien, the widow, and the orphan.
- Reflect on our Lord Jesus, who chose to leave the glories of heaven and become an alien in his own world, suffering abuse and discrimination. Because he chose to become an alien, no one needs to remain an alien. Thank you, Jesus!

Anger-restrainer

Yet he was merciful; he forgave their iniquities and did not destroy them. Time after time *he restrained his anger* and did not stir up his full wrath. He remembered that they were but flesh, a passing breeze that does not return.

—Ps 78:38–39

- Perhaps you can recall a time when you were so angry that you acted in a shameful way.
- If anyone has a legitimate reason to be angry, it is God. Every sin is ultimately a sin against him. Imagine how many sins are committed daily by the billions of people of the world. Then consider the restraint he shows by not lashing out and destroying every sinner.
- It takes more strength to restrain justifiable anger than it does to express it. God regularly chooses to restrain his anger when he is sinned against.
- Praise God for his restraint and his great love, which causes him to delay judgment on sinful people: "The Lord is not slow in keeping his promise, as some understand slowness. He is patient with you, not wanting anyone to perish, but everyone to come to repentance" (2 Pet 3:9).

Angry One

Moses heard the people of every family wailing, each at the entrance to his tent. The Lord became *exceedingly angry*, and Moses was troubled.

—Num 11:10

- Immediately after God disciplined Israel for complaining and grumbling against God, the people once again began to gripe. God is exceedingly angry at their ingratitude and rebellious hearts.
- Typically when we think of people who are "exceedingly angry," negative images come to mind. We think of raging, out-of-control people yelling, throwing things, or using profanity. God's anger is something else. It is calm, deliberate, controlled, and purposeful.
- Praise the Lord for his righteous anger. We would not want to live in a world where no one gets angry. When people choose to drive drunk, we want people to get angry. When children are forced into sexual slavery, we want people to get angry. When the powerful exploit the weak, we want people to get angry.
- Even our Lord Jesus got angry on occasion: "People were bringing little children to Jesus to have him touch them, but the disciples rebuked them. When Jesus saw this, he was indignant. He said to them, 'Let the little children come to me, and do not hinder them, for the kingdom of God belongs to such as these'" (Mark 10:13–14).
- Reflect on Jesus, who felt the full force of God's anger on the cross as he took our sins upon himself.
- Praise God that because of Jesus, we will never experience the anger of God.

Animal-lover

But the Lord said, "You have been concerned about this vine, though you did not tend it or make it grow. It sprang up overnight and died overnight. But Nineveh has more than a hundred and twenty thousand people who cannot tell their right hand from their left, *and many cattle as well*. Should I not be concerned about that great city?"

—Jonah 4:10–11

- Jonah hated the people of Nineveh and everything about them, and he was peeved that God would show them any kindness. It seems Jonah had a heart two sizes too small. He cared for no living thing in the Assyrian capital of Nineveh.
- The psalmist said, "the earth is full of your creatures" (Ps 104:24) and "these all look to you to give them their food at the proper time" (Ps 104:27) and "The lions roar for their prey and seek their food from God" (Ps 104:21).
- Too often in our world, we see animals only as "resources" to do with as we please, not as God's creations intended to glorify him.
- God cares for cows as well as people. Although not created in his image as we are, animals still have worth and should be treated with respect, whether kept as pets, raised for food, or admired in the wild.
- Proverbs 12:10a says, "A righteous man cares for the need of his animal."
- Praise God for his love and caring for animals.

Anointer

Now it is God who makes both us and you stand firm in Christ. *He anointed us*, set his seal of ownership on us, and put his Spirit in our hearts as a deposit, guaranteeing what is to come.

—2 COR 1:21–22

- Old Testament kings and high priests were anointed to signify God's blessing and set them apart for his service in a special way. Oil was poured on their heads, trickling down their faces and beards.
- Similarly, believers in Jesus Christ are said to be anointed in a figurative way, having been set apart by God for the work he has prepared for us to do. His favor is poured on our heads, just as these verses indicate.
- Praise God, who makes us stand firm in our faith, gives us his indwelling presence, and sets his special mark of ownership upon us. How blessed is every child of God!

Approachable One

In him and through faith in him we may *approach God* with freedom and confidence.

—Eph 3:12

- Sometimes we feel unworthy to approach someone famous or important, if only because we don't want to bother them. At other times the rich and the famous make it clear that they do not want to be approached.
- Even though none is greater, richer, more famous, or more important than God, he is approachable.
- Even though the Lord "lives in unapproachable light," we are invited to enter (1 Tim 6:16). Because we are his children through faith in Christ, we are urged to "approach the throne of grace with confidence, so that we may receive mercy and find grace to help us in our time of need" (Heb 4:16).
- Praise God for his approachability, and praise Jesus, who opened up a way for us to come into the presence of God without fear.

Arm-strengthener

I will *strengthen the arms of the king of Babylon*, but the arms of Pharaoh will fall limp. Then they will know that I am the Lord, when I put my sword into the hand of the king of Babylon and he brandishes it against Egypt.

—Ezek 30:25

- Many a boy has sought to build up his physique by lifting weights. We may be able to build up our arm muscles, but we are powerless to make the arms of others strong. We may long to be able to help strengthen the weak, but it is not within our power.
- What we cannot do, God can. If he wants a king to succeed and overcome his foe, he can make it happen. If he wants to make a strong person weak so he is unable to defend himself, he can just say the word, and it comes to pass.
- Praise God for his ability to make the weak strong, enabling the weakest of us to be strong enough to overcome every challenge or obstacle according to his good pleasure and purpose.

Arouser of the Wicked

The Lord aroused against Jehoram the hostility of the Philistines and of the Arabs who lived near the Cushites.

—2 Chr 21:16

- King Jehoram forsook the Lord, so the Lord punished him by arousing enemies to attack him.
- We may attempt, at times, to control people by manipulating them, but in the end, we are ultimately unable to control people or make them do what we want.
- Praise God that even wicked kings and nations must submit and do his bidding when he gives the command.
- Praise God, who has the last word in all things: "The Lord works out everything for his own ends—even the wicked for a day of disaster" (Prov 16:4).
- Reflect on the truth that sometimes God uses an unsaved person in our lives to teach us a needed lesson. Then praise God for his ability to direct all things to his will.

Attitude-changer

For seven days they celebrated with joy the Feast of Unleavened Bread, because the Lord had filled them with joy by *changing the attitude* of the king of Assyria, so that he assisted them in the work on the house of God, the God of Israel.

—Ezra 6:22

- After the destruction of the temple in 586 BC and the seventy-year exile, faithful Israelites returned to Jerusalem only to be met with the daunting task of rebuilding the temple in the face of opposition and limited resources. No problem. God simply prompted the king of the world-dominant nation to lend a helping hand.
- Many people struggle to change their attitude even when they know they should. How much more challenging is it to change the attitudes of others! Yet for God, this is child's play; he has the ability to change the attitude of anyone he chooses. What an amazing ability! What an amazing God!
- Praise God for his ability to change attitudes—mine as well as the attitudes of others in my life.

Author

You killed the author of life, but God raised him from the dead. We are witnesses of this.

—Acts 3:15

- Some writers receive large advances to write because they are either famous (retiring presidents, for example) or are already proven, successful authors.
- God is an author. He doesn't write books (although he did write one bestseller); rather, he is the author of something far greater. He is the author of life itself. What he "created" was not a work of fiction or history but life itself.
- Praise God, the author of life, who, ironically, chose to die so that dying people could have eternal life. Incredible!

Avenger

The Lord is a jealous and *avenging God*; the Lord *takes vengeance* and is filled with wrath.

—Nah 1:2

"It is mine *to avenge*; I will repay. In due time their foot will slip; their day of disaster is near and their doom rushes upon them"

—Deut 32:35

"O Lord, *the God who avenges, O God who avenges*, shine forth. Rise up, O Judge of the earth; pay back to the proud what they deserve"

—Ps 94:1–2

- There resides deep within us all a longing for the just punishment of those who arrogantly use, exploit, and abuse others. Countless movies have been made in which lawbreakers are relentlessly pursued and brought to justice by heroes who have a passion to see that the innocent are avenged.
- Praise God for his passion to bring about justice, ensuring that the wicked are called to account for their sins.

Awesome

Do not be terrified by them, for the Lord your God, who is among you, is a great and *awesome* God.

—Deut 7:21

- What comes to mind when you hear the word "awesome"? Perhaps a close-up view of Niagara Falls, or the Grand Canyon, or a mountain-top vista, or the birth of baby?
- Biblically, "awesome" has an element of fearsome might and power. When Israel was at risk of being terrorized by the inhabiting nations in the promised land of Canaan, God commanded them to not be terrified because he is far more terrible and awe-inspiring in all his power than they.
- Jesus told the disciples the same thing: "Do not be afraid of those who kill the body but cannot kill the soul. Rather, be afraid of the One who can destroy both soul and body in hell" (Matt 10:28).
- Praise the awesome God, for to fear him aright drains all other fears of their dread.

Beautiful

From Zion, perfect in *beauty*, God shines forth.

—Ps 50:2

- We tend to associate the word "beauty" with women, art, sunsets, or hitting a receiver in full stride with a forty-yard pass. Our culture is obsessed with physical beauty. Hollywood stars adorn the covers of magazines and electronic screens. Yet there is a beauty that lies beyond Hollywood's grasp—an inner beauty characterized by hearts that are loving, compassionate, selfless, good, and noble. Jesus displayed all these qualities perfectly in his daily life as he interacted with others. His was a beauty that attracted all people of goodwill.
- God has a beauty that is rivaled by none. When we see him, we shall be struck speechless by his radiant splendor.
- Praise God for his beauty. One day we shall see him and marvel.

Bestower of Favors

For the Lord God is a sun and shield; the Lord *bestows favor* and honor; no good thing does he withhold from those whose walk is blameless.

—Ps 84:11

- We often ask, "Can you do me a favor?" and by so doing we are asking for grace—for help undeserved.
- God delights in bestowing his favor on "those whose hearts are blameless." This does not mean that only sinless people qualify for God's favor (Who would qualify?), but rather that those who love him and love to please him by their glad obedience, however imperfectly executed, are favored.
- Reflect on the many favors God has bestowed on you by his grace and praise that he is the kind of God who is pleased to honor you.
- Has any greater favor been bestowed than Jesus, our Savior, and the gracious Holy Spirit, who indwells within us moment by moment? Praise the God who is the greatest favor of all.

Binder

Even though someone is pursuing you to take your life, the life of my master *will be bound securely* in the bundle of the living by the Lord your God. But the lives of your enemies he will hurl away as from the pocket of a sling.

—1 SAM 25:29

- Wise and beautiful Abigail, future wife of King David, declares to David that even though Saul pursues him, God will keep him safe because God has promised to do so (v. 30) using a wonderful image of being tied up securely in a bundle with all other living people.
- Praise God, who has a purpose and a plan for each life. He binds us snugly in the bundle of the living so we can fulfill our calling and complete our assigned work on earth. Then he will remove us from the bundle of the living and take us to heaven.
- Praise God that our lives are secure in Christ.

Binder

I will search for the lost and bring back the strays. *I will bind up* the injured and strengthen the weak, but the sleek and the strong I will destroy. I will shepherd the flock with justice.

—Ezek 34:16a

- God compares the leaders of Israel to shepherds and the people to sheep. He condemns these selfish, negligent, and abusive men for their failure to care for those in the land who are weak, defenseless, and abused.
- God declares that he will be their shepherd and he will see that his flock is cared for. He will bind up the wounds of the injured sheep and tenderly nurse them back to health.
- We are God's sheep, and Jesus is the Good Shepherd. It was prophesied of him, "The Spirit of the Sovereign Lord is on me, because the Lord has anointed me to preach good news to the poor. He has sent me to *bind up the brokenhearted*, to proclaim freedom for the captives and release from darkness for the prisoners, to proclaim the year of the Lord's favor and the day of vengeance of our God, to comfort all who mourn, and provide for those who grieve in Zion" (Isa 61:1–3a).
- Praise God for Jesus, the Good Shepherd, who cares for his sheep, binding up our hurts.

Bird-knower

I *know every bird* in the mountains, and the creatures of the field are mine.

—Ps 50:11

- "Are not two sparrows sold for a penny? Yet not one of them will fall to the ground apart from the will of your Father" (Matt 10:29).
- Birds are an amazing part of God's creation. The music that pours forth from some of the smallest of songbirds is enthralling. Their agility in flight, their plumage, and their habits are mesmerizing. How is it they do they not freeze to death in the cold winter snows? How do they fly so fast and then alight on a twig in a flash, without a wobble or a misstep?
- Have you ever wondered how many birds live within a five-minute walk from your home? Hundreds? Thousands? However many, God knows each one.
- God knows birds. Whereas in all our busyness, we may not take time to notice our surroundings, it is not so with God. He is on a first-name basis with every bird.
- God is not only a bird expert. He also knows every cow, cricket, and crocodile. What kind of a mind does God have to relate to all his creation in such detail?
- Praise God today for his creation and for the high value he places on all he has made, including humankind: "you are worth more than many sparrows" (Matt 10:30b).

Blesser

When God raised up his servant, he sent him first to you to *bless* you by turning each of you from your wicked ways.

—Acts 3:26

- Peter was preaching to a crowd that gathered after he and John healed a crippled beggar. He reminded these Jewish listeners of God's promise to bless all people on earth through his covenant with Abraham. Peter then stated that those who heard Jesus that day would be the first to be blessed by God through Jesus, who turned them from their sins to the Savior.
- Praise God, who is a blessing-giving God. He delights in bringing good to people.
- An old hymn encourages us to count our blessings. How long would your list be if you wrote out as many blessings as you could recall in the span of five minutes? We may be surprised by all the Lord has done!

Boldness-giver

Now, Lord, consider their threats and *enable* your servants to speak your word with great *boldness*.

—Acts 4:29

- Peter and John prayed this prayer to God after their release from arrest for preaching about Jesus. They were ordered to no longer preach in the name of Jesus.
- Threats by powerful people tempt us to be fearful. Realizing this, the disciples asked God to give them boldness, knowing they could not conjure boldness up within themselves.
- Parents at times wish for the ability to give boldness to their children as they try some new sport or venture. It is a hard, if not impossible task to give someone boldness.
- Praise God, the One who can and does give boldness to timid and fearful people. When we need it, we can ask him for it, and through the wonderful agency of his indwelling Holy Spirit, we are "enabled" to be bold.

Bread

Then Jesus declared, "I am the *bread of life*. He who comes to me will never go hungry, and he who believes in me will never be thirsty."

—John 6:35

- Bread comes in a variety of shapes and textures and is comprised of various grains, rice, or potato. It is a basic food staple in many cultures and has been called "the staff of life."
- If we want to live, we need to eat. What is true physically is also true spiritually. We need the Lord, the bread of life, to sustain us spiritually. He is "the bread that endures to eternal life" (John 6:27).
- Praise God for giving us Jesus, the staff of life.

Brother

Whoever does God's will is my *brother and sister and mother.*

—Mark 3:35

- While Jesus's birth family stood outside the house, Jesus made this amazing statement to those inside. Anyone who does God's will is considered a member of Jesus's own family. This is a staggering truth. Why would Jesus want us as members of his family? Yet he does.
- That means that all Christians are our siblings. Regardless of the size of our birth families, our spiritual family dwarfs them all.
- Praise God for including us in his family. How privileged we are!

Burden-bearer

Praise be to the Lord, to God our Savior, who daily *bears our burdens*.

—Ps 68:19

- In the movie *The Lord of the Rings: Return of the King,* Frodo the hobbit is called upon to carry a great burden—a destructive ring of power—to Mount Doom on a quest to destroy it before it falls into the hands of the evil Sauron. As he draws nearer to Mount Doom, Frodo finds his burden too great to bear. Seeing Frodo labor under the weight of the ring, his friend, Samwise Gamgee, carries Frodo's pack—and eventually Frodo himself, when his friend is no longer able to walk.
- The strong carry the burdens of the weak, whether by helping with a fellow hiker's pack or carrying a weary child.
- Praise God, who is our Burden-bearer. When we become weary and come to the end of our physical, emotional, or spiritual strength, we can look to God to bear our burdens.
- Reflect on Jesus, who bore our burden of sin on his shoulders on the cross.

Caller

But when God, who set me apart from birth and *called* me by his grace, was pleased to reveal his Son in me so that I might preach to the Gentiles, I did not consult any man.

—Gal 1:15–16

- Can you recall the moment when you came under strong conviction of your need for a Savior? The testimony of many is that they found themselves compelled from within to respond to the gospel message.
- God invites, calls, and even "commands all people everywhere to repent" (Acts 17:30b). Beyond this general call, there is another call from God that is more specific.
- Praise God for the amazing and yet mysterious way that he draws lost people to himself. Those who were spiritually blind, disinterested, and lost now see, become keenly interested, and are found! How sweet the sound of this amazing grace that saved such lost sinners as we.

Carrier

You yourselves have seen what I did to Egypt, and how *I carried you* on eagles' wings and brought you to myself.

— Exod 19:4

Like an eagle that stirs up its nest and hovers over its young, that spreads its wings to catch them and *carries them* on its pinions.

—Deut 32:11

- Throughout North America, the bald eagle is making a comeback. It is an increasingly common sight to see an eagle in majestic flight.
- God compares himself to a great eagle and us to baby eaglets. Just as an eagle can swoop under an eaglet that founders in flight, so the Lord swoops down to catch us when we are either unable to fly or lack the confidence to do so. We all fall at times and need the strong wings of God to swoop under us to lift us up and keep us from harm.
- Praise the God who catches and carries us when we stumble or fall.
- Praise the Lord Jesus, who was willing to fall to his own great hurt on the cross so that we would be lifted up to safety.

Celebrator

But we had to *celebrate* and be glad, because this brother of yours was dead and is alive again; he was lost and is found.

—Luke 15:32

- Families celebrate people, events, and milestones—things like birthdays, new jobs, births, graduations, last student loan payments, etc.
- We have a God who celebrates. As the father in the story of the lost brothers (better known as the Parable of the Prodigal Son), God declares that "we had to celebrate and be glad." Just as our homes ring with the joy and laughter of celebrations, so does God's in heaven when even one sinner repents and comes home.
- Jesus said, "there will be more rejoicing in heaven over one sinner who repents than over ninety-nine righteous persons who do not need to repent" (Luke 15:9).
- Reflect on our celebrating God and his rejoicing over us when we come to faith.

Changeless

But you *remain the same*, and your years will never end.

—Ps 102:27

- It is hard to think of anything in this world that does not change. It is the nature of things to do so. Well, not all things.
- God is both timeless and changeless. He is Mr. Dependable in a world of fickleness and forgetfulness. As he was when we first knew him, so is he now and will be forever.
- Reflect on the reliability and dependability of God and his words in the Bible in contrast to the world around us.
- Praise God, the timeless and changeless one to whom we can anchor our lives.
- Reflect on the Lord Jesus, the very same Jesus who walked this earth, and consider how thrilling it will be to see him face-to-face in heaven.

Chastener

The Lord has *chastened* me severely, but he has not given me over to death.

—Ps 118:18

- God delivered the psalmist into and out of the hands of an enemy, and in so doing, helped him learn the lesson of humility.
- God's love causes him to chasten us—to not only correct us when we go astray, but also to train us to be godly. His tools of chastening can include trying circumstances, disappointment, sickness, and hardship.
- Just as good parents discipline and teach their children with consequences, so does God with his children. He is transforming us into the likeness of his Son, Jesus, and chastening us is one of the means he uses.
- Praise God that his love prompts him to chasten us as he sees fit.
- "My son, do not despise the Lord's discipline and do not resent his rebuke, because the Lord disciplines those he loves, as a father the son he delights in" (Prov 3:11–12).

Chariot-owner

The chariots of God are tens of thousands and thousands of thousands; the Lord has come from Sinai into his sanctuary.

—Ps 68:17

- See also 2 Kgs 6:8–17.
- The chariots of old were the tanks of modern warfare. Infantrymen respect the advantage tanks give on the battlefield.
- If we were to talk about God's might in military terms, we would need to replace chariots not with tanks but with the most technologically-advanced weapons system known to man. God is the only military super-power.
- Reflect on the Almighty power of God and praise the One whose power protects and keeps us.
- Consider the Lord Jesus, who will one day judge and make war against all nations that wickedly oppose God, bringing final and complete justice. Astride a white horse, he will lead the armies of heaven to victory (Rev 19:11–21).

Chooser

If you belonged to the world, it would love you as its own. As it is, you do not belong to the world, but I have chosen you out of the world. That is why the world hates you.

—John 15:19

- Many a child has experienced the dread of waiting to be chosen for a pick-up game by the gifted (and often self-appointed) captains. Each child hopes for the honor of being chosen first and, barring that, hopes against hope not to suffer the indignity of being chosen last.
- In the upper room, Jesus told the disciples that he chose them. Surely they recalled how he, after a night of prayer, selected the Twelve from a larger group of disciples.
- Every Christian is a chosen person. In the mystery of God's sovereign ways, his Spirit stirred our deadened spirits and called us to come. We gladly heeded that call.
- Praise God that he chose us to be his daughters and sons. God has no "minor leagues" when it comes to our value or place in his family—each of us has been chosen first by our Captain. We are cherished and loved. Reflect on this truth and then march out with confidence to meet the day.

City-watcher

Unless the Lord builds the house, its builders labor in vain. Unless *the Lord watches over the city*, the watchmen stand guard in vain.

—Ps 127:1

- Picture a vigilant watchman pacing the ramparts of ancient Jerusalem, scanning the horizon for any hint of the enemy's approach. Regardless of how alert he is or how quickly he sounds the alarm, the city will fall unless the Lord has determined that it will stand.
- Unless God says so, it will be impossible for any city to stand—or fall. Even if the enemy is strong and has superior forces, it will not prevail without God's permission.
- Praise God, the watchman of the city of our lives. Our confidence is in him for safety and protection. Of course we are to watch our lives closely (1 Tim 4:16 tells us, "Watch your life and your doctrine closely. Persevere in them, because if you do, you will save both yourself and your hearers"), but ultimately our trust is in God and his ability to keep us and our loved ones from all harm.
- Let the truth of this verse saturate our minds today: "If God is for us, who can be against us?" (Rom 8:31b). If God is not for us, it doesn't matter who is for us.

Cloud-rider

He *makes the clouds his chariot* and rides on the wings of the wind.

—Ps 104:3b

There is no one like the God of Jeshurun, who rides on the heavens to help you and *on the clouds* in his majesty.

—Deut 33:26

- Through the marvel of computer-generated imagery, it appears that people can do anything—fly, become invisible, display super-human strength, breathe under water, and more. We know that this is fantasy, but we are entertained nevertheless.
- But there is One who can do such things. God can do anything he wants, and the image here is of God planting his feet on the clouds and riding across the skies. Written in a time when flight was considered only a cartoonish fantasy and beyond the wildest imaginations of men, this image spoke of God's boundless abilities.
- Praise the God of the impossible. Nothing is too hard for him.
- Fix your eyes on Jesus, who ascended into the clouds and who will one day come back in the same way (Acts 1:9, 11).

Comforter

Praise be to the God and Father of our Lord Jesus Christ, the Father of compassion and the God of all comfort, *who comforts us* in all our troubles, so that we can comfort those in any trouble with the comfort we ourselves have received from God.

—2 Cor 1:3–4

- Most of us have found ourselves struggling to know how to comfort someone in grief. How we wish we could say or do just the right thing that would take away their pain. Some wounds will not fully heal this side of heaven.
- God is compassionate and a Comforter, so much so that he is called "the Father of compassion." His heart is soft towards those who grieve and toward those who are overwhelmed by life's troubles. He cares for the brokenhearted.
- Praise God, who "is full of compassion and mercy" (Jas 5:11).

Commander of Angels

For he will *command his angels* concerning you to guard you in all your ways.

—Ps 91:11

- Many of us give little thought to angels. Neither do we spend much time thinking about the devil or his demonic horde, for that matter.
- We would believe in angels and demons and the reality of Satan and would have no doubt that they are powerful and awe-inspiring if we could but see them as they truly are.
- Praise God, the Commander of all the angels—the good ones and the bad ones. If it pleases him to send an angel on a mission, he goes without hesitation. If he assigns an angel to protect us or our loved ones, we are protected. If God needs an evil spirit to do his bidding, even it must yield and do as he commands.
- We rejoice in our safety because of God's legions of angels who daily protect us.
- Reflect on the fact that our Lord Jesus could have called legions of angels, all poised to do his bidding, when he hung on the cross, but he chose to stay there for our sake.

Commander of Nature

In fear and amazement they asked one another, "Who is this? *He commands even the winds and the water*, and they obey him."

—Luke 8:25b

When I shut up the heavens so that there is no rain, or *command locusts* to devour the land or send a plague among my people.

—2 Chr 7:13

- A popular series of movies was based on seemingly ordinary people who had the power to command wind, water, fire, or storms because they had supposedly evolved to the next level of humanity. While we know existence of such X-Men is pure fantasy, it is entertaining to imagine having these kinds of abilities.
- God actually has such powers. Jesus displayed them in his life when he calmed the wind and the waves in the storm on the Sea of Galilee. And unlike the X-Men, Jesus was not restricted to one power—he is master of all powers. Animals do God's bidding, as Noah undoubtedly discovered, for the animals presented themselves at God's bidding to book passage (Gen 6:20).
- Reflect on the truth that all things yield to God's will. Every living thing harkens to his voice and obediently carries out his wishes, as does the very creation itself. We need fear no thing, no person, no force of nature—for they are God's to command.

Companion

The Lord is *with me*; I will not be afraid. What can man do to me? The Lord is *with me*; he is my helper. I will look in triumph on my enemies.

—Ps 118:6–7

- One of the names given to Jesus was Emmanuel, meaning "God with us." From the time of the tabernacle and temple of the Old Testament to the coming of Jesus and the gift of the indwelling Holy Spirit, a theme of the Bible is that God wants to be with us.
- Praise God for his continued presence with all who trust in Christ. Not only are we never alone, but the One with us is none other than God Almighty, with all his power and might. No one can touch us without God's say-so. We are invincible until he removes his protecting hand from our lives.
- Praise our abiding God: "Jesus replied, 'If anyone loves me, he will obey my teaching. My Father will love him, and we will come to him and make our home with him'" (John 14:23).
- Rejoice that God promises, "Never will I leave you; never will I forsake you" (Heb 13:5b).

Compassionate

As a father has *compassion* on his children, so the Lord has *compassion* on those who fear him.

—Ps 103:13

The Lord is gracious and righteous; our God is full of *compassion*.

—Ps 116:5

- Every parent understands what it is to suffer with someone. When our children fall and hurt themselves, our hearts are touched and pained. When they taste disappointment or failure, we feel their pain. Their suffering is our suffering.
- Our God understands our suffering, for he chose to suffer with us— and to identify with our pain. What a wonder that our God would choose to suffer with us—and for us, as our Lord Jesus did on the cross.
- Reflect on the Lord's tender-heartedness for his children. Praise him for his compassion for a lost, sinful world.

Confidence

For the Lord will be your *confidence* and will keep your foot from being snared.

—Prov 3:26

For you have been my hope, O Sovereign Lord, my *confidence* since my youth.

—Ps 71:5

- Many people struggle with a lack of confidence. And maybe with good cause. We know our limitations and our true selves better than anyone, and what we know may not cause us to overflow with confidence. It is only by God's grace that we have made it this far in life without making a greater mess of things.
- It is tempting to place our confidence in all kinds of things—money, abilities, job, another person, or ourselves. But each of these can fail us or be taken away. Then what?
- Praise God, who cannot fail nor be taken from us. This truth, coupled with God's commitment to us, gives us daily confidence regardless of our circumstances.
- The Apostle Paul lived with confidence in God. He said, "I can do everything through him who gives me strength" (Phil 4:13) and "If God is for us, who can be against us?" (Rom 8:31b).

Confronter

> Woe to you Pharisees, because you give God a tenth of your mint, rue, and all other kinds of garden herbs, but you neglect justice and the love of God. You should have practiced the latter without leaving the former undone.
>
> —Luke 11:42f

- Our Lord Jesus saved his harshest words for the religious leaders of his day for their failure to live out the core teachings of God in the Scriptures. He fearlessly confronted them and exposed their sin.
- Most of us do not like confrontation, but sometimes it is necessary. Confronting can actually be an expression of love, even if the one receiving it does not take it that way. James said, "Remember this: whoever turns a sinner from the error of his way will save him from death and cover over a multitude of sins" (Jas 5:20).
- Praise God that he loves us enough to confront us when we stray so we can remain in a place where God can bless us.

Consoler

When anxiety was great within me, *your consolation* brought joy to my soul.

—Ps 94:19

- It was said of the mothers in Bethlehem, whose young children were murdered by the paranoid King Herod, "A voice is heard in Ramah, weeping and great mourning, Rachel weeping for her children and refusing to be comforted, because they are no more" (Matt 2:18).
- What can we say to a mother at such a time? How do we console a broken heart? Words fail us.
- It is not only the grieving who need consolation. The worriers and the uptight also need it. At times anxious thoughts flood our minds and paralyze us.
- How grateful we are to have a consoling God. Because Jesus lived on this earth, he understands exactly what we face and is thus able to comfort and encourage us in times of distress.
- Reflect on the consoling words of God in the Bible and the One who extends them to us.

Cord-cutter

But the Lord is righteous; he has *cut me free from the cords* of the wicked.

—Ps 129:4

- Samson, the Old Testament judge, was bound with cords by his enemies after his deceitful wife, Delilah, discovered and divulged the secret to his great strength.
- Not all cords are physical. We are warned in the Bible about the unseen cords that seek to wrap themselves around us: "the sin that so easily entangles" (Heb 12:1b).
- Praise God, our cord-cutter. Through Jesus' death on the cross, God has freed us from the binding power of sin, and now he helps us throw off everything that hinders us and the sin that so easily entangles.

Counselor

You guide me with your *counsel*, and afterward you will take me into glory.

—Ps 73:24

- A list of counselors can be found in the Yellow Pages and online. Some are good, others less so. Even the best of them are not always entirely successful in helping those who seek counsel.
- One of the prophetic titles given to Jesus was "Wonderful Counselor" (Isa 9:6).
- Praise God for sending us two Wonderful Counselors: our Lord Jesus and, after his ascension, another Counselor—our constant companion and indwelling guide, the Holy Spirit. Remember, "But the Counselor, the Holy Spirit, whom the Father will send in my name, will teach you all things and will remind you of everything I have said to you" (John 14:26).
- Praise God, our Counselor, whose wisdom and knowledge are available to us through the Bible and his gracious Spirit.

Covenant-maker

For this reason Christ is the mediator of *a new covenant*, that those who are called may receive the promised eternal inheritance—now that he has died as a ransom to set them free from the sins committed under the first covenant.

—Heb 9:15

- God is a covenant-making God. He made covenants with Adam, Abraham, Noah, David, the people of Israel—and with us. He always keeps his stipulations, even while we struggle to hold up our end. Even so, he continues to faithfully bind himself to us in these wonderful covenant relationships so that we might be blessed.
- Praise God for his commitment to us as displayed in his new covenant, sealed by nothing less than the precious blood of Christ, a lamb without blemish or defect.
- Praise God that our inconsistencies and sins do not cause him to give up on us.
- Praise God for his decision to take upon himself the penalty for our covenant violations. How gracious and merciful!

Covenant-rememberer

He *remembers his covenant* forever, the word he commanded, for a thousand generations.

—Ps 105:8

- We tend to forget all kinds of things—people's names, places, appointments, what we promised, phone numbers, and more.
- The United States government has made many treaties with First Nation peoples over the past two hundred years, most of which have been forgotten. To our shame, we are a forgetful people.
- God's covenant with Christians promises several things: "I will put my laws in their minds and write them on their hearts. I will be their God, and they will be my people. No longer will a man teach his neighbor, or a man his brother, saying, 'Know the Lord,' because they will all know me" (Heb 8:10b–11).
- Reflect on the reality that God is not a forgetful God. When he makes a promise, he keeps it. A thousand generations may come and go, but he remembers his covenant with us.

Coverer

He *will cover you* with his feathers, and under his wings you will find refuge; his faithfulness will be your shield and rampart.

—Ps 91:4

- It is amazing how many chicks can squeeze under the wings of their mother. When the mother hen sounds the alarm, they hurry under her protective shelter until the all-clear is sounded.
- Praise God that we vulnerable "chicks" can flee to him, finding a safe haven under his wings. Whereas a mother hen may be unable to protect her sheltered chicks from all danger (an attacking fox, for example), God's wings are much stronger; no predator will prevail against him.
- Praise God that he is always close by and that we can find refuge under his wings.

Craftsman

For we are *God's workmanship*, created in Christ Jesus to do good works, which God prepared in advance for us to do.

—Eph 2:10

- It is amazing what gifted craftsmen can produce. Shapeless blocks of stone or wood are sculpted into works of art. Old dilapidated houses are transformed into modern, attractive homes. Craftsmen create that which is both pleasing and functional. They don't make junk.
- God is the finest Craftsman. He takes the base material of our lives and transforms it into something beautiful and useful for his glory and service. Just as people admire a craftsman's handiwork, so we ought to strive to be the kind of people who reflect favorably on our Master Craftsman.
- Praise God that even though we are still under construction, we are confident of the end product: "being confident of this, that he who began a good work in you will carry it on to completion until the day of Christ Jesus" (Phil 1:6).

Creator

Do you not know? Have you not heard? The Lord is the everlasting God, the *Creator* of the ends of the earth. He will not grow tired or weary, and his understanding no one can fathom.

—Isa 40:28

- Humankind has created some amazing works of art, architecture, and technology. In this way we reflect God, the Creator of all things.
- Humankind's creations pale in comparison to what the Lord has made. This world is amazingly complex and wondrous. Whether we turn our eyes to the small parts of God's creation (molecular) or to the large parts (a universe choked with galaxies), we are amazed at what God has created. And the most mind-boggling aspect of this is that God had no materials to start with! Building the Millennial Falcon from Legos is one thing, but creating a tree or a mountain from nothing is something else entirely. God is amazing!
- A magician can produce a dove seemingly out of thin air. and when he does, people applaud and ooh and aah. How can we not be more impressed with the One who produced a universe from nothing!
- Reflect on God's creation, and ponder the Genius who made it all.

Cross-bearer

Carrying his own cross, he went out to the Place of the Skull [which in Aramaic is called Golgotha].

—JOHN 19:17

- Mel Gibson's movie, *The Passion of the Christ*, is powerful and disturbing. The depiction of the violence of crucifixion in ancient Rome was sobering, sickening, and realistic. Death on a cross was intended to shock and sicken those who watched as a deterrent to law-breaking.

- Praise the Lord Jesus, who carried his cross to Golgotha—not because he had no choice, but rather because he did have a choice. He was not out of options. This was the option he chose. Rome's military was not strong enough to compel him to be crucified against his will. He chose to carry the cross. He chose to suffer. He chose death—this particular kind of death. He volunteered for this suicide mission. Why would anyone do that? We know the answer. Because of his love for us and for his desire to display the gracious nature of the God who made us. This is a shake-your-head kind of amazing.

Crowner

Who redeems your life from the pit and *crowns you* with love and compassion.

—Ps 103:4

- When Peter, Edmund, Susan, and Lucy were crowned at the end of C. S. Lewis' *The Lion, the Witch, and the Wardrobe,* they were honored as the kings and queens of Narnia. Despite being children, they were anointed as royalty.
- Praise God, the One who alone deserves to wear a crown, who yet chooses to crown us with love and compassion. May we wear this love, richly bestowed upon us through the Lord Jesus, like a crown. May the awareness of God's kindness and compassion settle on our heads and heart today, reminding us of his greatness.

Curdler

Did you not pour me out like milk and *curdle me like cheese*, clothe me with skin and flesh and knit me together with bones and sinews?

—JOB 10:10–11

- The making of cheese is an intentional, multi-step process in which the cheese-maker transforms milk into a product of his liking, shaping it into a block or a wheel.
- Job declares that just like the potter, the cheese-maker invests time and effort into making his product. Job understands that God's work in his life is like that of the cheese-maker, in that God is involved in a process Job neither understands nor likes. He wonders why the great Cheese-maker would go to all the bother of making cheese of his life only to have him suffer and die. Job struggles with the "why" question.
- God brings various pressures upon us as part of the processes of life's circumstances for purposes that are often as unclear to us as they were to Job. It is by faith that we understand that "And we know that in all things God works for the good of those who love him, who have been called according to his purpose" (Rom 8:28).
- Praise God, who is making something good out of our life circumstances.

Curse-bearer

For it is written: *"Cursed is everyone* who does not continue to do everything written in the Book of the Law ... Christ redeemed us from the curse of the law by *becoming a curse for us,* for it is written: "Cursed is everyone who is hung on a tree."

—Gal 3:10b, 13

- In Western cultures it is uncommon for people to believe in curses. They seem to be so *unscientific* somehow. But clearly God believes in them.
- Deuteronomy 27 describes a scene where, on two opposing mountains, the twelve tribes of Israel crowd the summits. From one peak the words ring out, "Cursed is the man who ... cursed is the man ... cursed is the man." Twelve times a curse is declared on any person who fails to keep the agreed-upon covenant. Meanwhile, on the other mountain, echoing words of blessing are issued for those who choose to obey the covenant.
- All who sin violate God's law and fall under the curse of judgment outlined in God's Law. The wages of our sin is death, and God pays his wages on time and in full.
- Praise God for the Lord Jesus, our Curse-bearer, who chose to be cursed so that we might be blessed. That calls for a standing ovation and a round of applause! Actually, it calls for a life of humble service as an expression of our gratitude.

Defender of Widows

A father to the fatherless, *a defender of widows*, is God in his holy dwelling.

—Ps 68:5

- In biblical times, certain members of society were vulnerable to exploitation by the powerful and the rich. Widows were among that group.
- God has a special place in his heart for those who cannot defend themselves—widows, orphans, and aliens are mentioned often.
- Praise God for his love and concern for those who have no one to turn to but God when in need. This concern reveals his heart and the kind of person he is.
- "Religion that God our Father accepts as pure and faultless is this: to look after orphans and widows in their distress and to keep oneself from being polluted by the world" (Jas 1:27).

Delighter

The Lord detests men of perverse heart, but *he delights in those whose ways are blameless.*

—Prov 11:20

- Most of us know the feeling of joy and delight when we see a loved one after a long absence or meet a distant friend.
- Just as we know that experience, so too does God express delight in certain people.
- It is both humbling and sobering to realize that we have the ability to bring pleasure and joy to God. Who are we that we should have any effect upon God? But truth be told, he finds pleasure in us when we live our lives according to his commands. How humbling to be so honored!
- Reflect on God, who delights in those whose hearts are right with him. May the thought of his smiling face looking down on you bring you joy today.

Deliverer from Graves

But God will *redeem my life from the grave*; he will surely take me to himself.

—Ps 49:15

- People usually don't choose to picnic in a cemetery; it is a place of sadness, sorrow, and painful memories.
- A part of the good news of the gospel is that Jesus could not stay dead in the tomb, and because we are united with him, we will not stay dead in our graves: "because we know that the one who raised the Lord Jesus from the dead will also raise us with Jesus and present us with you in his presence" (2 Cor 4:14).
- Praise God that the redemption price has been paid for our release from the grave and from death. We have "crossed over from death to life" (John 5:24), and thus we "will never see death" (John 8:51). We need not live in fear of death or of what comes after, for God will "surely take me to himself." We can even picnic in a cemetery if we want, because we know that death has lost its terror.

Deliverer

Reach down your hand from on high; *deliver* me and rescue me from the mighty waters, from the hands of foreigners.

—Ps 144:7

The Lord who *delivered me* from the paw of the lion and the paw of the bear will deliver me from the hand of this Philistine.

—1 Sam 17:37a

- David testified that just as God helped him overcome attacks from a lion and a bear, so too will he deliver David from Goliath, the Philistine giant.
- It is safe to say that most of us have never wrestled a bear or a lion, nor have we ever faced off against a nine-foot man on the field of battle. But David did, and despite the odds, David, the underdog, won—not because of luck or years of training but because of God.
- Praise God, who is able to deliver us from any and all danger. He can—and will—deliver us from the lions, bears, and giants in our lives, according to the master plan he has for our lives: "And lead us not into temptation, but deliver us from the evil one" (Matt 6:13).
- Praise the Lord Jesus, who delivered himself into the hands of his enemies so that we might be delivered from the clutching hands of death and hell.

Demon-caster

Jesus was driving out a demon that was mute. When the demon left, the man who had been mute spoke, and the crowd was amazed.

—Luke 11:14

- Satan's work in our world varies according to what he believes is most effective. Obvious demonic possession is not a tactic he uses in most Western cultures. He prefers to work more stealthily there, it seems.
- God is King and Master not only of the good angels in heaven, but also of the fallen angels in this world (and those he has already locked up—see Jude 6) who seek to do us harm.
- Praise God for his mastery over the spiritual powers. When he tells them to go, they must go. And when he tells them to leave us alone, they do so. And since the authority of Jesus has been given to us, we have the same power to command demons to get out of our way and leave us alone.

Demon-master

Now the Spirit of the Lord had departed from Saul, and *an evil spirit from the Lord* tormented him.

—1 Sam 16:14

The next day *an evil spirit from God* came forcefully upon Saul.

—1 Sam 18:10a

- Dualism is a wrong way to think about the relationship between God and Satan. They not equally powerful opposing powers that balance each other out in the world. Satan does what he does only by God's permission. He is the proverbial mad dog on a chain that is restrained by God's mighty hand and will. There is an element of mystery in how all that works out, but the Bible is clear that all things are under God's masterful control, including Satan and his hosts.
- Praise God for his right and power to use all things, including evil spirits, for his purposes. If he needs an evil spirit to punish a persistently wicked person, for example, then he can and does. There is no competing power that can frustrate God's plans.
- Praise God that even when the world seems to be spinning out of control, it is not. God is master of all, including of the godless and the demonic, and his plan is unfolding right on schedule. That gives us peace and confidence to face the day.

Desire-giver

Delight yourself in the Lord and he will *give you the desires of your heart*.

—Ps 37:4

You open your hand and *satisfy the desires* of every living thing.

—Ps 145:16

- This is a wonderful promise—God will give us the desires of our heart. But it comes with a condition. If we meet the condition, then we shall reap the promise. If God is our delight, if our highest pleasure is his will and glory, then he will grant us that which our hearts desire. Even when our prayers are answered with a "no," this promise is still valid, for when we truly want what God wants, we gladly set aside our request for his better plan.
- Jesus affirmed this promise when he said, "But seek first his kingdom and his righteousness and all these things will be given to you as well" (Matt 6:33).
- Praise God, our Desire-granter. Whereas we are powerless to grant even our own desires, God is able to grant the desires of millions.

Destroyer

He will repay them for their sins and *destroy them* for their wickedness; the Lord our *God will destroy them.*

—Ps 94:23

- Mad dogs and rabid animals must be destroyed because they are irretrievably corrupted. Can the same thing can happen to people? Is it possible that those who give themselves over to persistent sin, refusing to repent, can get to the place where they are irretrievably corrupted? Sadly, it is so. Sin is not static—it progresses.
- Praise God that no corrupting or poisonous influence will be allowed in heaven.
- Let us rejoice that there is a place where the irretrievably wicked will be kept so they do not again rebel against God.
- Praise God that although we were once counted among the rebels, his grace has redeemed us and is extended to all who will lay down their arms and surrender to God, the King.

Director

May the Lord *direct your hearts* into God's love and Christ's perseverance.

—2 Thess 3:5

- A director of a play positions people on stage according to the script.
- In baseball, a manager positions the outfielders according to who is up to bat.
- God has the wondrous ability to direct our hearts so they are where they ought to be for us to experience God's love and perseverance in doing right despite threats from Satan (vv. 3–4).
- Praise God for his mysterious workings in our hearts, moving, prompting, and directing us so that we are blessed and strengthened. May our hearts be tuned to his presence and the inner workings of the Holy Spirit.

Discernment-giver

I am your servant; *give me discernment* that I may understand your statutes.

—Ps 119:125

- Some people are gifted with the ability to intuitively read people based on body language, voice inflection, and other subtle cues.
- We wish for the power of discernment, both for ourselves and for others. There are too many unscrupulous people in the world, and it would be nice to be able to identify who they are so we could avoid being taken advantage of.
- Praise God for his ability to give discernment to those who need it. He gives insights into others, into our own hearts, into the Scriptures, and into the inner voices we hear.

Disciplinarian

My son, do not despise *the Lord's discipline* and do not resent his rebuke, because the Lord *disciplines* those he loves, as a father the son he delights in.

—Prov 3:11–12

- See also Heb 12:4–13.
- Most of us can recall times when our parents disciplined us after we had done something wrong. We may not have liked it, but we realized (perhaps not until later) they meant it for our own good.
- To correctly understand what God means by discipline, we need to get rid of the idea that discipline is punishment. Discipline is training, either by rules and regulations, rewards, life circumstances, life experiences, or, when necessary, by chastisement.
- Praise God for his correcting love, which trains us to be godly. Every hour of every day, he is working in us to transform us into the likeness of his Son.

Disgrace-remover

Take away the disgrace I dread, for your laws are good.
—Ps 119:39

- Can you imagine what it would be like if people could read our minds? If our every thought were projected on a screen for all to see, we would indeed be red-faced. We may not necessarily indulge or invite those thoughts, but they come rushing in nonetheless. One of our daily exercises is to persistently push them back out.
- We may never have experienced public disgrace, but we realize that if our inner thoughts were known, that would soon change.
- Praise God, who has taken away our disgrace. Our past sins, with their attendant shame and disgrace, have been forgiven and washed away, never to be held against us. How wonderful that once we come to God in Christ by confession, repentance, and faith, our disgrace is gone.
- Praise Jesus, the one person who never committed a shameful act or had a sinful thought, who nevertheless allowed our shame to be heaped upon him on the cross. How we ought to love him!

Dismantler

Since they show no regard for the works of the Lord and what his hands have done, he will *tear them down* and never build them up again.

—Ps 28:5

- There are those who make their fortunes through dishonesty and theft. Not all thieves wear masks; some wear suits and ties. For those who don't care who they hurt in order to profit and get ahead, the Lord has a message: your day of reckoning will come. Jesus spoke of the rich man who foolishly built bigger barns to hold his excess grain only to discover that he was going to die soon and would enjoy none of his wealth.
- Praise God that a day of tearing down is coming for those who get ahead by cheating others. They may be able to skirt and manipulate the law, but they will not escape God. Lord, help us not to envy the wicked and the wealthy.
- "Do not let your heart envy sinners, but always be zealous for the fear of the Lord" (Prov 23:17).

Displayer of His Holiness

Therefore say to the house of Israel, "This is what the Sovereign Lord says: It is not for your sake, O house of Israel, that I am going to do these things, but for the sake of my holy name, which you have profaned among the nations where you have gone. *I will show the holiness of my great name*, which has been profaned among the nations, the name you have profaned among them. Then the nations will know that I am the Lord," declares the Sovereign Lord, "when I *show myself holy* through you before their eyes."

—Ezek 36:22–23

- There is a story of a lazy and drunken soldier named Alexander who served in Alexander the Great's army. He was brought before the king, who told him, "Either change your name or change your conduct." The king did not want dishonor brought to the name of Alexander.

- Just as Alexander wanted to protect the dignity of his name, so God wants to protect the dignity of his. He opposes all things that are wrong and sinful. If a widow is exploited, he opposes it. If a spouse is cheated on, he opposes it. If a man's reputation is damaged by lies, he opposes it. If the God of the universe, who is good, holy, and worthy of applause is disrespected, then he opposes that too. It is a matter of consistency.

- Praise God for his holiness and for his desire to display and protect the holiness of his name. It is a good thing that God cares for his reputation, knowing that if he is portrayed as weak, unholy, unjust, or unloving, an injustice would be done. God is to be admired for his intent to protect his good name.

DISPLAYER OF HIS HOLINESS

- Praise God for Jesus, who lived a life of complete holiness before a watching world, enabling us to see what holiness looks like when it is lived out in daily life.

Doer of the Immeasurable

Now to him who is *able to do immeasurably more* than all we ask or imagine, according to his power that is at work within us, to him be glory in the church and in Christ Jesus throughout all generations, for ever and ever! Amen.

—Eph 3:20–21

- What comes to mind when you think of immeasurable things? The number of water drops in the ocean? The number of grains of sand in the Sahara? The number of stars in the universe or cells in the human body? Despite our vast advancements in science, some things just cannot be measured—we can only estimate and guess.
- Praise God for his immeasurable power and ability. When it comes to asking and imagining what God could do in our lives, through our lives, and in the lives of others around us, we often think small.

Door-opener

And pray for us, too, that God may *open a door* for our message, so that we may proclaim the mystery of Christ, for which I am in chains.

—Col 4:3

- The doors to our houses provide access to our homes or open up a world of opportunity as we step out of them.
- When we speak of an open door, we think of options and opportunity; we have a chance to try something new.
- A "door-opener" is an opportunity-maker. God opens doors of opportunity for us when we are stuck or trapped by circumstances.
- Reflect on the fact that God is able to open doors of all kinds, including doors of the heart, opportunities to serve, witness, encourage, and more. Paul says that God responds to prayers when we ask for him to open up doors for us.

Dragger

Do not *drag me away* with the wicked, with those who do evil, who speak cordially with their neighbors but harbor malice in their hearts.

—Ps 28:3

- In the movie *Ghost*, starring Patrick Swayze and Demi Moore, when wicked people die, demon-like shadowy figures rise up through the ground to drag them away as their prey kicks and screams in terror.
- When you hear of people being dragged away, what image comes to your mind? Police arresting criminals? Guilty defendants exiting the courtroom?
- How do you feel knowing that God has the power and the will to drag evil people away to judgment?
- Praise God that the wicked will be held accountable for their choices. Praise him that God will bring every wicked person to justice and judgment.
- Rejoice that wicked sinners who put their hope and trust in God through Jesus Christ will never be dragged away but will instead be escorted into heaven in a triumphant procession. Reflect on how good God is to do this for us.
- Ponder the Lord Jesus, who allowed himself to be dragged away by the wicked so as to ensure that we will never be dragged away.

Drawer

No one can come to me unless the Father who sent me *draws him*, and I will raise him up at the last day.

—JOHN 6:44

- In the physical world, God created certain drawing forces. Magnets exert a strong pull on certain metals. Gravity draws all objects downward.
- In the spiritual realm, there is a drawing power, lovingly exerted by God upon the human soul, which inexorably moves people toward God and his redeeming grace.
- Praise God for his mysterious drawing power. He gently and lovingly woos and draws humanity to himself. It is a power that people do not share.
- Praise Jesus, who proclaimed that God's redeeming love was extended to all people, Jews and Gentiles alike: "But I, when I am lifted up from the earth, will draw all men to myself. He said this to show the kind of death he was going to die" (John 12:32–33).

Ear-turner

I love the Lord, for he heard my voice; he heard my cry for mercy. Because *he turned his ear to me*, I will call on him as long as I live.

—Ps 116:1–2

- We tend to tune out sounds that are unimportant to us, while those sounds that are important catch our ears. Avid birdwatchers ask, "Did you hear that?" We heard nothing, but they detect a songbird in the distance.
- Like us, God's ear is tuned to sounds that are important to him. Among them are the cries of his children.
- When we are in trouble and pray to God, his ear, like that of a mother who can single out her own baby's cry in a room full of crying babies, is so attuned to our voices that he will turn his head, see us in need, and come to our aid.
- Because the Lord heard the psalmist's plea for rescue and delivered him, the psalmist declared his lifelong loyalty to God. An appropriate response.
- Praise God for his constant awareness of and attention to his needy children.

Enabler

The Sovereign Lord is my strength; he makes my feet like the feet of a deer, he *enables* me to go on the heights.

—Hab 3:19

- Habakkuk wrote these words at a time when the economy was in shambles and people (himself included) were in desperate financial straits. Despite these circumstances, Habakkuk declared that God enabled him to rise above them. Habakkuk used the analogy of a nimble deer on the mountain heights to describe what God did for him.
- Praise God that he can enable us to overcome anything we face in life while we trust in him.
- Rejoice that God is not some cosmic drill sergeant whose demands leave us demoralized. God is gracious and kind, enabling us to do what he calls us to do.

Encourager

May the God who gives endurance and *encouragement* give you a spirit of unity among yourselves as you follow Christ Jesus, so that with one heart and mouth you may glorify the God and Father of our Lord Jesus Christ.

—Rom 15:5–6

- People who encourage others are a rare breath of fresh air. They have a knack for seeing the positive at hand and picturing the potential that might be. They are not blind to the weakness and immaturity in others but choose rather to focus on the potential.
- Praise God, our Encourager, who while keenly aware of where we need to grow, does not dwell on our shortcomings. He encourages us by telling us what we will do and will become as we surrender to him and are filled with his Holy Spirit: "I can do everything through him who gives me strength" (Phil 4:13).
- Even when we go through hardship, we are to be encouraged because hardship is one of the ways that God lets us know of his love for us; he is treating us like sons and daughters (Heb 12:4–13).

Endurance-giver

For everything that was written in the past was written to teach us, so that through *endurance* and the encouragement of the Scriptures we might have hope. May *the God who gives endurance* and encouragement give you a spirit of unity among yourselves as you follow Christ Jesus, so that with one heart and mouth you may glorify the God and Father of our Lord Jesus Christ.

—Rom 15:4–6

- How wonderful would it be to be able to give endurance to those we know who are weary and worn down by their struggles? But alas, we do not have the ability to give such a wondrous gift.
- God suffers from no such inability. He gives endurance to people! He enables us to persevere through the most devastating of circumstances, overcoming seemingly insurmountable obstacles.
- Praise God, who encourages us with his promises in the Bible, reminding us that he will either remove the source of our struggles or make us stronger so that we will overcome them.
- Praise God too for his encouraging presence—we are never left alone.

Enemy-lover

But *love your enemies*, do good to them, and lend to them without expecting to get anything back. Then your reward will be great, and you will be sons of the Most High, because he is kind to the ungrateful and wicked.

—Luke 6:35

- Loving our enemies goes against our human nature. We love those we like and we love strangers in need, but our hearts do not go out to those who hate and hurt us.
- God loves his enemies. He does not treat them as they deserve but chooses instead to be kind to them and seeks to bless them. Ultimately, he hopes that love will conquer the hateful heart and bring about repentance.
- While we were enemies of God (Rom 5:10), he loved us by sending his Son so we could be made into friends—more than that, into family!
- Praise God for his love for those in his family and even for those who choose to remain outside it.

Engraver

See, I have engraved you on the palms of my hands; your walls are ever before me.

—Isa 49:16

- Some tradesmen etch their names in the metal of their tools so they can identify their property if it were to be borrowed or lost.
- In stressing to his people, Israel, that he would never forget or abandon them, God uses this same imagery. He engraves them on his hands so that he will see them often during the day and be reminded of them. Some people today do the same thing—they tattoo the names of their children or loved ones on their arms as a permanent way of remembering them.
- Praise God for his willingness, as it were, to tattoo our names on his hands as a way to remember us. Of course, God does not need reminders as humans do, but he uses an image we can identify with to make his point. We are in a covenant relationship with God, and he will never forget us.
- Praise God for Jesus, whose hands will be marked for eternity by the prints of the nails that held him to the cross. The nail-prints on his hands will serve as reminders of us as well.

Enricher

You will be made rich in every way so that you can be generous on every occasion, and through us your generosity will result in thanksgiving to God.

—2 Cor 9:11

- Paul is encouraging the Corinthian Christians to be generous with their money in contributing to an offering to be set aside for fellow believers in need. He reminds them that if they are generous, they will find that God is more generous. He will give them more so they can give even more.
- The world's way of creating wealth is by working hard, investing wisely, winning the lottery, or by becoming the favored child of a rich uncle!
- How we would love to be able to make people rich—family members who struggle with debt, single moms, widows on fixed incomes, and others impoverished by life's circumstances—but we are unable to do so because of our limited resources.
- God's resources are not limited, for he is immensely wealthy. He owns everything, and he generously gives his riches to people as he pleases.
- Praise God for his generous heart and for his wisdom in giving according to what is best.

Enthroned One

The Lord sits *enthroned* over the flood; the Lord is *enthroned* as King forever.

—Ps 29:10

- Few kings or queens oversee kingdoms from their thrones any longer.
- God is King over a kingdom, and he watches over it from his throne. Nothing that takes place in his kingdom escapes his watchful eye, and he governs with a firm and just hand.
- Praise God, our King, and give thanks that we have the privilege of living in a kingdom with such a loving and just sovereign.
- Rejoice in the King, who sits on his throne, overseeing his great kingdom and overseeing the tiny kingdoms of our lives.

Eternal

The *eternal* God is your refuge, and underneath are the everlasting arms.

—Deut 33:27a

- We say, "Nothing lasts forever," but that is not quite true. Much in this world ages, wears out, is torn down, or dies, but God neither ages nor has an expiration date. He created time and stands outside it, totally unaffected by its impact on all created things.
- Praise God that he will never get old, retire, be replaced, or change. He is eternally dependable, loving, good, and just.
- Praise God that even though we are not eternal (we have a beginning), we are offered eternal life through Christ Jesus—life without end. Soon this life will be past, and we shall live with the God who loves us.

Ever-present One

And surely I am *with you always*, to the very end of the age.

—MATT 28:20B

- Jesus gave this assuring promise to his disciples before he ascended into heaven. Although he would no longer be visibly present with them, he would still be invisibly present with them by means of the Holy Spirit.
- Extended separation from loved ones produces loneliness and sadness, as does having no earthly family at all.
- Jesus is the constant companion of every Christian and the friend from whom it is impossible to be separated. We can open our hearts to him safely knowing he loves us, cares for us, and is able to help us.
- Praise God for his constant presence and for his promise that nothing can separate us from his love (Rom 8:35–39).
- See also Ps 139

Examiner

The Lord is in his holy temple; the Lord is on his heavenly throne. He observes the sons of men; *his eyes examine them*. The Lord *examines the righteous*, but the wicked and those who love violence his soul hates.

—Ps 11:4–5

- Tests given by teachers and professors are called "examinations." They are tools to look inside each student and measure his or her level of knowledge and understanding.
- God's scanning eye examines us. He peers into our inner person to assess each of us.
- Praise God that his all-seeing eye is trained on us for our good. He uses the information he gathers to benefit us—to help us grow in the likeness of Christ. Praise him that he knows when we tried to do the right thing even if it comes out all wrong. Praise him too that he can see damaging sin lurking in the recesses of our hearts and draws it out through trials and testing so we can work with him to remove it.

Executioner

See now that I myself am he! There is no god besides me. *I put to death* and I bring to life. I have wounded and I will heal, and no one can deliver out of my hand.

—Deut 32:39

- In this Song of Moses, God declares that he will bring judgment on all enemies who defy and challenge him or his right to rule his world.
- All humankind resides under the judgment of God in the sense that we all will die. But those who defy God while they live expose themselves to the risk of a more immediate and terrible judgment. Truly, "It is a dreadful thing to fall into the hands of the living God" (Heb 10:31).
- Praise God that his righteous anger against our sin has fallen on Jesus on the cross, so there is no longer any condemnation for us.
- Praise God that even when we stumble as Christians, we will never face the wrath of God, because we are now sons and daughters of God.
- Praise God that we are safe in the hands of Jesus and God the Father, and "no one can deliver" us out of that safe haven.

Exerciser

This is what the Lord says: "Let not the wise man boast of his wisdom or the strong man boast of his strength or the rich man boast of his riches, but let him who boasts boast about this: that he understands and knows me, that *I am the Lord, who exercises* kindness, justice, and righteousness on earth, for in these I delight," declares the Lord.

—Jer 9:23–24

- A dictionary definition of exercise is "an act of employing or putting into play; use."
- When we exercise our bodies, we put them into action—into use.
- When God exercises kindness, justice, and righteousness, he is putting them into play, much as a coach would insert new players into the game.
- Praise God for his many past kindnesses and for his many promises of future kindness to us.
- Praise God for his justice. One day, all wrongs will be made right, and each person shall receive his or her reward.
- Praise God for his righteousness. He always does what is right, good, and holy.
- Let our boast today be that we know this wonderful God, and that he has set his affection upon us.

Eye-opener

Open my eyes that I may see wonderful things in your law.

—Ps 119:18

- Can you imagine what it would be like to lose your sight? All of life would be radically and forever changed.
- As much as we value our physical sight, our spiritual sight—the ability to peer into that unseen, eternal realm—is far more precious.
- Jesus demonstrated that God can make blind eyes see. He healed the physically blind, but praise God, he is equally able to open our spiritual eyes.
- Praise him for opening our eyes to see our sin, and for the Savior who died for those sins.
- Praise God for enabling us to see his truth in the Bible.
- May our eyes be open to see wonderful things today in his Word.

Eye-ranger

For the eyes of the Lord range throughout the earth to strengthen those whose hearts are fully committed to him.

—2 Chr 16:9a

- If our forefathers were told it would be possible for a satellite to effortlessly float above the earth taking pictures of people on the ground, they would have been incredulous. If they had been told that this "eye in the sky" would also be able to communicate with us through our wireless phones no matter where we go, they would think it a joke.

- God is the original "Eye in the Sky": he who scans the world, keeping an eye on all the people who love him, and giving them the strength they need to do their work. He is also able to communicate with us at any time and in any place.

- Praise God that his eye is on us all the time and that he can infuse us with strength to live out our days in a way that is pleasing to him.

- Praise him that our prayer messages (and millions of others simultaneously) can fly back and forth between him and us at remarkable speed. What a great God!

Eye-turner

Turn my eyes away from worthless things; preserve my life according to your word.

—Ps 119:37

- We are surrounded by worthless things. We are constantly bombarded with graphic, crude, and sinful images through television and other media. How can a person maintain a pure heart and mind under this relentless barrage?
- God can help us. He has the power to help us turn our eyes from these seductive images and temptations. We know that we are weak and vulnerable and need help to say no to worldliness and ungodly passions (Titus 2:11–12)
- Praise God for his ability to help us turn our eyes away from worthless things and to fix our eyes on that which is true, noble, right, pure, lovely, and admirable.
- As we turn our eyes from the worthless things of this world, let us, like the psalmist, replace those worthless images with something more worthy—thoughts of our Lord Jesus: "Let us fix our eyes on Jesus, the author and perfecter or our faith, who for the joy set before him, endured the cross, scorning its shame, and sat down at the right hand of the throne of God" (Heb 12:2).

Face-shiner

Make your face shine upon your servant and teach me your decrees.
—Ps 119:135

- When we see someone we love, our faces light up, expressing our joy and delight.
- When God's face shines on us, it means that he is pleased with us and that we have his favor and acceptance.
- Praise God for his shining face toward us today. Praise him that we don't need to be perfect in order to receive his favor and acceptance.
- Throughout the day today, picture God's smiling face looking down upon you.

Faithful One

For great is your love, reaching to the heavens; your *faithfulness* reaches to the skies.

—Ps 57:10

- Regrettably, many promises and vows to be faithful are broken or set aside because those making them no longer wish to honor them.
- When God makes a vow, he never breaks it, nor does he ever grow weary of keeping it. He has made a covenant—a binding agreement—with all who will repent towards God and put their faith in Christ Jesus (Acts 20:21).
- If faithfulness were a brick, then God's faithfulness would be a tower that pierces the clouds.
- Praise God for his faithfulness to us and for his determination to abide by all the promises he made to us through Christ.

Faith-giver

Immediately the boy's father exclaimed,
"I do believe; *help me overcome my unbelief!*"

—MARK 9:24

- The father of this boy ached over the torment his young son endured due to an evil spirit. He had surely exhausted every potential source of healing but found none. In his discouragement, he doubted that even Jesus could help. Yet Jesus said, "Everything is possible to him who believes" (v. 23). The father wanted to believe, but his faith was small.
- Jesus helped this man's unbelief in a wondrous way—he delivered the boy from his tormenter!
- Praise God for his help in overcoming our doubts and our weak faith.
- Praise God that we are not saved by our own pumping up of our small faith into something bigger, but rather that we are saved by God's grace through the slender conduit of faith that connects us to him.

Famine-sender

He called down famine on the land and destroyed all their supplies of food.

—Ps 105:16

- God needed to get Jacob and his family to Egypt so he could display his power by confronting and defeating the gods of Egypt. After sending Joseph on ahead to get things set up, God then stopped the rain for a few years, destroying all the food supplies in Canaan by means of a famine.
- Why? God wanted to provide the world and his people, Israel, a dramatic demonstration of his power so they would love him, remain faithful to him, and, in time, produce the Savior who would die for the sins of the world.
- Praise God for his occasionally unorthodox methods for working out his plan among us.

Father

This, then, is how you should pray:
"Our *Father* in heaven, hallowed be your name."

—Matt 6:9

- Fathers come in all forms—good, bad, absent, consistent, strict, etc.
- No one has ever had a perfect father, yet we all know what a perfect father looks like.
- Praise God, our heavenly Father. He is the epitome of the perfect father, loving us and working in our lives, always to grow us into his likeness, expressed most perfectly in the life of Jesus.

Father to the Fatherless

A *father to the fatherless*, a defender of widows, is God in his holy dwelling.

—Ps 68:5

- Millions of children in the world are orphans, having neither father nor mother. Some are abandoned and have no one to care for them.
- God has a particular concern for the weak and defenseless, often charging us to be his agent of relief and care.
- Praise God for his tender heart and his concern for those who have been robbed of their fathers and mothers. With God, there are no "throw-away children."

Feeder

How many are your works, O Lord! In wisdom you made them all; the earth is full of your creatures ... These all look to you to *give them their food* at the proper time. When you give it to them, they gather it up; when you open your hand, they are satisfied with good things.

—Ps 104:24, 27–28

- God providentially provides food for the numberless creatures of the earth.
- Jesus said that birds neither sow nor reap, nor store away in barns, and yet God feeds them.
- Praise God for his care and provision for all his creatures, great and small.
- Praise God for his provision for us, for we are his creatures as well. Not only does he give us our daily bread, but he feeds our spiritual hunger as well.

Fever-lifter

The royal official said, "Sir, come down before my child dies." Jesus replied, "You may go. Your son will live"... When he inquired as to the time when his son got better, they said to him, "The fever left him yesterday at the seventh hour."

—JOHN 4:49–50A, 52

- Who among us would not love to have the power to heal every sick person we meet? Sadly, such power eludes us.
- But God has the power. He made our bodies, and he knows how to fix them.
- When we get sick, often our first thought is to call for a doctor for treatment. Surely God does much healing through the agencies of medical professionals; they apply the treatment, and God does the healing.
- God has the power to instantly heal any affliction—fevers, cancers, even death—and we should ask him to do so even as we work with his agents, our doctors.
- Praise God for his power to heal, at times instantly, at other times gradually, and sometimes by taking us to heaven.

Fighter

The Lord will fight for you; you need only to be still.

—Exod 14:14

- Israel was terrified to find the Egyptian army closing in as they stood defenseless on the shores of the Red Sea. Moses reassured his people that they had nothing to fear because God was going to fight for them.
- Often when we are being pursued or attacked, our response is to panic, give in to fear, or to fight back. Sometimes God would have us defend ourselves, but other times we need to trust God to deal with our attackers in his own time and way.
- Praise God that we do not need to fight our battles alone—and that at times we don't need to fight our battles at all. All we need do is be still and trust God.
- Praise God for Jesus, who fought and defeated sin, death, Satan, and hell for us.

Fire

For the Lord your God is a consuming *fire*, a jealous God.

—Deut 4:24

- Images of out-of-control forest fires are awe-inspiring as they consume all in their path.
- God's possessive love is compared to such a fire.
- As Israel was poised to enter the promised land, Moses warned them that God's possessive love could be compared to a raging fire. Since Israel was pledged to God in a covenant relationship, they needed to avoid the sin of idolatry because God would not stand by while his people pursued other gods. He jealously protects what is his.
- Praise God for his holy, jealous love and for his passionate determination to see that nothing separates us from him.

Fire-master

He makes winds his messengers, *flames of fire his servants.*

—Ps 104:4

- Humanity has made fire its servant. Controlled fire heats our homes, cooks our food, and toasts our marshmallows for s'mores. But at times, fire breaks out and burns down our forests, our homes, and sometimes even us.
- God is the master of the winds that swirl around our planet and the flaming lightning bolts in the storm-filled sky.
- Praise God for his mastery of not only the winds and the waves, but also of the bolts of flame that yield to his will.

Food-provider

He *provides food* for those who fear him; he remembers his covenant forever.

—Ps 111:5

- Part of God's covenant with Israel was that he would bless their land, trees, flocks, and herds so that there would be an abundance of food and resources.
- Praise God for his practical ability to provide food for those he loves.
- Praise God for his covenant with us through Christ Jesus, wherein we are promised every provision, including food: "But seek first his kingdom and his righteousness, and all these things will be given to you as well" (Matt 6:33).
- Of course, God may choose for us to experience a lack of resources for a time, but even this deprivation is under his watchful direction and in fulfillment of his purpose.

Foot-setter

You have not handed me over to the enemy
but have *set my feet* in a spacious place.

—Ps 31:8

- Every parent desires to set their children's feet on a path in life that is safe, happy, blessed, and filled with all that is good.
- But we do not have the means to direct our own footsteps, let alone those of our children and grandchildren.
- Yet the psalmist believes that God has kept him from the hands of his enemy and has providentially set his feet in a good and spacious place.
- In another psalm, David said that God "lifted me out of the slimy pit, out of the mud and mire; he set my feet on a rock and gave me a firm place to stand" (Ps 40:2).
- Praise God, who is charge of setting our feet in good and spacious places, according to his good pleasure.

Foot-steadier

For you, O Lord, have delivered my soul from death, my eyes from tears, *my feet from stumbling*, that I may walk before the Lord in the land of the living.

—Ps 116:8–9

- Physically, stumbling is a risk for the frail and elderly, for those walking in the dark, and for those who are weary. Figuratively, we can stumble with our words, in our resolve, or in our decision-making.
- God is able to deliver us from both kinds of difficulties. Like the psalmist, we can look back and see God's gracious hand delivering us from death, heartache, or stumbling in some way.
- As we reflect on how God has delivered us in the past, let us praise him for the assurance that he will continue to deliver us, as we trust in him.
- Praise him too for Jesus, who stumbled under the weight of the cross so that our feet could be placed on solid ground.

Footstep-director

Direct my footsteps according to your word; let no sin rule over me.

—Ps 119:133

- A blind person needs help to avoid obstacles and pitfalls, or else they will be injured.
- Similarly, we need someone to direct our steps in life so that we are not harmed.
- God can tell us how to walk so as to avoid the sin that seeks to rule over us. It is the Bible ("according to your word") that God uses to tell us how to live in such a way that we avoid harm; the better we know it, the less likely we are to get off track and risk a fall.
- Praise God for his direction in the past and for his promised direction in the future.

Foot-washer

After that, he poured water into a basin and began to *wash his disciples' feet*, drying them with the towel that was wrapped around him . . . "I have set you an example that you should do as I have done for you."

—JOHN 13:5, 15

- In the first century, foot-washing was a humbling, menial task that was assigned to slaves and servants. It was a necessary task but a thankless one.
- When Jesus washed his disciples' feet, he demonstrated his love for them by doing whatever was necessary to serve their needs. This revealed Jesus' open heart toward them—and us.
- Reflect on what it says of God that he would love us enough to wash our feet. We agree with Peter that it is we who ought to wash Jesus' feet, not the other way around. What an amazing God, who honors us so!

Forgiver

*The Lord our God is merciful and *forgiving*, even though
we have rebelled against him.*

—Dan 9:9

- In answering Peter's question about how many times a person could be expected to forgive a brother (Matt 18:21–22), Jesus said seventy-seven times, or seventy times seven.
- Forgiving someone who sins against me a few times seems reasonable, but seventy-seven times—or 490 times! How is that possible? By following God's example.
- How many times have we sinned against God in word, thought, and deed or failed to do what we should? Surely 490 times pales in comparison to the number of our own offenses.
- As we reflect on the mound of our sins, let us praise God for the mountain of his grace expressed through his forgiveness.
- Praise Jesus for his selfless sacrifice for us so that we could be reconciled to God and experience his forgiveness.

Fortress

He is my loving God and *my fortress*, my stronghold and my deliverer, my shield, in whom I take refuge, who subdues peoples under me.

—Ps 144:2

- America is littered with forts, preserved from our nation's beginnings.
- A fortress is a place of safety, strategically located, well-defended, and hopefully impregnable, so that all who gather within will be kept safe from the enemy's attack.
- God is our fortress. When we are attacked, we do not need to retreat to a physical location, but rather the fortress comes to us. When we go to him in prayer and call upon him to shelter us, he is present until the danger is passed.
- Praise God for his ability and desire to shield us from harm in times of danger and attack.

Fragrance-spreader

But thanks be to God, who always leads us in triumphal procession in Christ and through us *spreads everywhere the fragrance* of the knowledge of him.

—2 Cor 2:14

- Long before fragrances came in expensive bottles with French-sounding names, they were found on blossoming bushes and flowers.
- God is spreading a fragrance throughout the world. The good news of the gospel message about Jesus is filling the earth just as surely as the scent of hyacinth fills a room.
- Praise God for his desire to bless all the peoples of the world with the fragrance of the gospel. Thank him for wafting that scent our way so we could become his children.

Freedom-giver

It is for freedom that *Christ has set us free*. Stand firm, then, and do not let yourselves be burdened again by a yoke of slavery.

—Gal 5:1

- Occasionally news stories tell of hostages who have been freed from captivity. Though haggard and weary, the captives are thrilled to be free. Their joy often steals the spotlight from the heroes of the story—those who brought about their release.
- Jesus is our hero. He orchestrated a daring and imaginative rescue of prisoners who had been locked up by sin (Gal 3:22). Through the marvel of the incarnation and his substitutionary death on the cross, Jesus freed us.
- Praise Jesus for his daring rescue and for his great love.

Friend

You are my friends if you do what I command. I no longer call you servants, because a servant does not know his master's business. Instead, I have called you *friends*, for everything that I learned from my Father I have made known to you.

—JOHN 15:14–15

If you have nothing in life but a good friend, you are rich.

—MICHELLE KWAN, *THE WINNING ATTITUDE: WHAT IT TAKES TO BE A CHAMPION*

- Jesus chose twelve men to be his inner circle of friends, men with whom he could share his hopes and plans. He kept nothing back from them concerning who he was or what he planned to do. He looked to them for support and encouragement, but he found them slow to grasp the big picture of God's plan.
- Reflect on the fact that the eternal God, creator of all things, calls us his friends. Calling us servants makes sense, as would employees perhaps, but friends? How honored we are!
- Praise God that he is willing to have people like us as his friends.

Fruit-grower

But the *fruit of the Spirit* is love, joy, peace, patience, kindness, goodness, faithfulness, gentleness, and self-control.

—Gal 5:22–23

- Picking apples at an orchard is an annual tradition in many families across some parts of the United States. Row upon row of trees bend under the weight of abundant McIntoshes, Cortlands, and Red Delicious apples.
- Just as the orchard owner tends the trees throughout the year so they can produce a crop, so God the Spirit tends our spirits all year long, producing in us a fitting crop.
- Praise God for the silent and mysterious inner work of his Spirit in our lives.
- Praise God for Jesus, who perfectly displayed each of these fruits when he walked this earth.

Frustrater of the Wicked

The Lord watches over the alien and sustains the fatherless and the widow, but he frustrates the ways of the wicked.

—Ps 146:9

- When Balak, a king of Moab, hired Balaam to curse the people of God, God continually frustrated the sinful prophet's efforts (Num 22–24).
- God has the power to frustrate, delay, stop, or redirect the plans of the wicked.
- Praise God that even though the wicked prosper at times, God can and will, if it so pleases him, prevent them from carrying out their plans or enjoying the fruit of their ill-gotten gains.
- Ask with confidence for God to frustrate the plans of those who hinder God's work or his people.

Gate

I am the gate; whoever enters through me will be saved. He will come in and go out, and find pasture.

—John 10:9

- Gates come in all shapes and sizes, but they have one purpose—to grant access.
- Praise God for the access that has been opened to us through Jesus. We now can approach God's throne of grace with confidence (Heb 4:16).
- When we enter through the narrow gate, we shall find all we need ("pasture") provided for us by the Good Shepherd.
- Praise God that the gate is open to anyone who desires to enter.

Gift

Jesus answered her, "If you knew *the gift of God* and who it is that asks you for a drink, you would have asked him and he would have given you living water."

—John 4:10

- Gifts mark special occasions in our lives. We give birthday gifts, Christmas gifts, and wedding gifts. In speaking to the woman at the well, Jesus was alluding to himself as God's gracious gift to her and to the world.
- A gift is a grace. The recipient does not pay for it, nor has he or she earned it as a reward.
- Praise God for the gift of inestimable worth we have been offered in Jesus, our Savior, Lord, and Friend.

Gift-giver

For it is by grace you have been saved, through faith—and this not from yourselves, it is *the gift of God*—not by works, so that no one can boast.

—EPH 2:8–9

- God is the creator, and we are the created. God is great, and we are small. God is holy, and we are sinful. If anyone should be giving gifts, it should be us giving gifts to God.
- But God is a gift-giver. Our salvation is given to us as a gift, not because we are gift-worthy but because it is the nature of the Gift-giver to give. That God offers us forgiveness speaks to the greatness of his heart, not to our worthiness. It is grace.
- Praise God for his gift-giving nature and for his supreme gift, his Son, Jesus Christ: "For God so loved the world that *he gave* his one and only Son, that whoever believes in him shall not perish but have eternal life" (John 3:16).

Giver of Eternal Life

I give them eternal life, and they shall never perish; no one can snatch them out of my hand.

—John 10:28

- Imagine having the power to restrain the ravenous specter of death from our lives and from those we love. How we wish we could give to our children the gift of an endlessly good life without the prospect of aging, accident, or sickness. Alas, we cannot.
- But God has that power, and he offers this very gift to us and to our children.
- Eternal life is life without end, but it is more than that. Eternal life is literally life of the age to come—a new kind of life—the heavenly life. This new life is infused into us when we come to Christ and put our faith in him. This new kind of life means we will never die (John 5:24; 8:51), even when our bodies grow too weak to sustain us.
- Praise God for his gift of eternal life. Praise him for the fact that no matter what our lives are like now, we will soon enjoy a new life that will be glorious without end.
- Praise Jesus, who gave up his glorious life in heaven so we could have eternal life.
- "For God so loved the world that he gave his one and only Son, that whoever believes in him shall not perish but have eternal life" (John 3:16).

Giver of Undivided Hearts

Teach me your way, O Lord, and I will walk in your truth; *give me an undivided heart*, that I may fear your name.

—Ps 86:11

- The first of the Ten Commandments is to have no other gods besides God. Some things are never meant to be shared or divided. The supremacy of God in our affections is one of those things.
- The world is full of idols, all of which compete for the affections of our hearts. We must be ever-vigilant to keep our hearts from being divided.
- For example, Jesus warned, "You cannot serve both God and money" (Matt 6:24b).
- The psalmist recognized that God can help us in our desire to maintain an undivided heart.
- Praise God for his ability to guard and strengthen our faltering hearts so that we never leave our first love: "Yet I hold this against you: You have forsaken your first love" (Rev 2:4).

Giver-overer

Hear, O my people, and I will warn you—if you would but listen to me, O Israel! ... But my people would not listen to me; Israel would not submit to me. So *I gave them over* to their stubborn hearts to follow their own devices.

—Ps 81:8, 11–12

- Sometimes, as a last resort, a parent will step aside and allow a stubborn and rebellious teen to have their way, knowing that the decision will lead to pain and heartache. They hope that their child will then realize their error and the folly of their ways.
- God, at times, does the same thing with his children. When he does this for a stubborn Christian, it is always motivated by love and for use as a teaching tool. When he does this for a stubborn non-Christian, it can be either a loving act or an expression of his judgment (see also Rom 1:24, 26, 28).
- Praise God for this expression of the hard side of his love to his children and for his judgment on those who will not repent.

Glorious Name

If you do not carefully follow all the words of this law, which are written in this book, and do not revere this glorious and awesome name—*the Lord your God—the Lord will send fearful plagues on you and your descendants, harsh and prolonged disasters, and severe and lingering illnesses.*

—Deut 28:58–59

- God's name in Hebrew is Yahweh, which is translated as LORD in English translations. It is the most intimate and personal name for God in the Old Testament. It means, "He is" when we speak of him and "I am" when God refers to himself.

- Just as our names refer to who we are as people, God's name refers to who he is. Since he is the greatest being that exists, he is entitled to honor and respect. The covenant arrangement between God and Israel stipulated that he be treated with proper respect, and if Israel failed to do so, significant penalties would be assessed.

- Reflect on God's nature and character and how he is a being filled with glory and splendor. When we see him in heaven, we will be awestruck at his greatness.

- Praise Jesus, "the exact representation" of God's being (Heb 1:3), whom the Father has exalted "to the highest place and gave him the name that is above every name, that at the name of Jesus every knee should bow, in heaven and on earth and under the earth, and every tongue confess that Jesus Christ is Lord, to the glory of God the Father" (Phil 2:9–11).

God of Gods

For the Lord you God is *God of gods* and Lord of lords, the great God, mighty and awesome, who shows no partiality and accepts no bribes.

—Deut 10:17

- Have you ever wondered who is Doctor to the doctors, President of presidents, and Judge of the judges? And whom do the gods look to as their God? It is the Lord God of the Bible, who is master of all and who is the boss of all beings, real and imagined, spiritual, and material.
- Praise God that there is only one God and that all powers and beings must and will bow before him. Recognizing this, we willingly and gladly bow before him now. Eventually all will do so, by force if necessary.
- Praise our God, who, although great and mighty, condescends to be our Father.

Grace-abounder

And God is able to *make all grace abound* to you, so that in all things at all times, having all that you need, you will abound in every good work.

—2 COR 9:8

- Paul reminds the Corinthian Church that when they are generous in supporting God's work, God responds by making grace abound to them.
- Grace is undeserved favor and unearned kindness.
- God has ways of bestowing blessings of all kinds, including financial (v. 10), on those whose love for God prompts them to give "generously" (v. 6).
- God does not scrimp and just give some; he gives "*all* grace . . . in *all* things at *all* times, having *all* that you need."
- Praise God for his promise of abundant grace to us in all its forms—financial, physical, spiritual, etc.—enabling us to "be made rich in every way so that you can be generous on every occasion" (v. 11).
- Praise God for Jesus, the supreme example of God's abounding grace. He was the best heaven had, and it was not held back from us in our need.

Gracious

Rend your heart and not your garments. Return to the Lord your God, for he is *gracious* and compassionate, slow to anger and abounding in love, and he relents from sending calamity.

—Joel 2:13

- The prophet Joel urges Israel to not merely show outward signs of repentance and humility before God but to make them truly heartfelt.
- It is possible to act in a gracious manner even when the heart is not gracious. Our motive can sometimes be joyless duty or a desire to impress or even to curry favor. God wishes for us to have our gracious actions stem from a gracious heart.
- God not only shows grace, his very essence is one of grace. He shows grace to us because his heart is gracious. His motives are never tainted by sin or selfishness.
- Praise God for his gracious heart, and be mindful of it when you stumble. Rejoice that we can go to him without fear and dread because we have seen his heart, and it is gracious and compassionate.
- What does a gracious life look like? Read the gospel accounts of Jesus, who was "full of grace and truth" (John 1:14b).

Grandchild-blesser

But from everlasting to everlasting the Lord's love is with those who fear him, and his righteousness with *their children's children.*

—Ps 103:17

- Perhaps God has providentially blessed you with children and grandchildren. It is pleasing to think that the kindness God has shown us will spill down to our children and then to their children.
- We pray for our children and our grandchildren to "fear him"—that is, to reverentially and humbly submit to God, placing their faith in Christ so as to experience the love of God that is "from everlasting to everlasting."
- Praise God for his great love poured out on our families, cascading down through the generations, "showing love to a thousand generations of those who love me and keep my commandments" (Exod 20:6).

Griever

How often they rebelled against him in the desert and *grieved him* in the wasteland!

—Ps 78:40

The Lord was grieved that he had made man on the earth, and his heart was filled with pain.

—Gen 6:6

- If you have lost a loved one to death, you know the emotional pain that accompanies such a loss. It is hard to describe to someone who has not yet experienced it.
- Is it not an amazing thing that God would allow the people he created to hurt him? And yet, that is just what he has done. Our sin grieves God's heart.
- When Jesus lived on the earth, he too experienced grief and sadness. He understands when we feel such pain.
- Praise God that he chooses to identify with us so fully that he is willing to walk with us in our sorrow and pain and help us through it.

Guardian

Guard my life, for I am devoted to you. You are my God; save your servant who trusts in you.

—Ps 86:2

- We are familiar with various kinds of guards—security guards, prison guards, and even guard dogs. Their job is to protect things of value, whether they be people or property.
- It is a sad reality in this fallen world that there are evil people and evil forces that prey upon others. We need guarding. Praise God, we have a Guardian.
- God stands guard over every believer. He is ever-vigilant, and he never sleeps or grows careless in the execution of his self-assigned duty. We are told that God commands his warrior-like angels to watch over us, protecting us from the enemy of our souls—Satan: "For he will command his angels concerning you to guard you in all your ways: they will life you up in their hands, so that you will not strike your foot against a stone" (Ps 91:11–12).
- Praise God, who guards us day and night.

Guide

For this God is our God for ever and ever; he will be our *guide* even to the end.

—Ps 48:14

- For those who live in rural states, the word "guide" brings to mind those men and women who guide out-of-state hunters seeking to bag a deer, moose, or bear. These guides undergo serious study and rigorous testing in order to be certified as a state guides. A certified guide instills confidence in those who hire them. When the hunt is over, the guide's work is done.
- God is our Guide. Not just for a week but for every day—"even to the end." Just as a knowledgeable guide instills confidence, how much more ought we to be at peace knowing that our Guide is the all-knowing and all-powerful God?
- Praise God that each day he goes before us: "he leads me beside the quiet waters, he restores my soul. He guides me in the paths of righteousness for his name's sake" (Ps 23:2b–3). Not only does he guide our feet, he guides our thoughts, conversations, and decisions as we listen to his Holy Spirit.

Hair-counter

Are not five sparrows sold for two pennies? Yet not one of them is forgotten by God. Indeed, the very *hairs of your head are all numbered*. Don't be afraid; you are worth more than many sparrows.

—Luke 12:6–7

- It has been said (by bald men, most assuredly) that God only made so many perfect heads. The rest he covered with hair.
- We are of such worth to God that he knows about the smallest and most seemingly insignificant details of our lives.
- Life can be scary, and we can feel all alone. But Jesus told us we don't need to be afraid because God has not forgotten us. We are of great worth to him, so he is not going to abandon us or forget about our needs.
- Praise God for his detailed watchfulness over us and for valuing us so highly.

Hand-holder

Yet I am always with you; you *hold me by my right hand*.

—Ps 73:23

- Parents of toddlers hold their children's hands when there is any risk of them falling or stepping off the sidewalk into traffic.
- The psalmist was at risk of falling away from his faith because he could not understand God's ways. Despite his confusion, the psalmist was convinced that God still kept a firm hold of his hand.
- As we picture God holding our hands, let us praise him for his loving care and attention, which exceeds that of any doting parent.
- Ponder the words of Jesus, who said that he was going to prepare a place for us: "and if I go and prepare a place for you, I will come back and take you to be with me that you also may be where I am" (John 14:3). Every time a Christian dies, this statement is fulfilled. Perhaps when Jesus comes to take us to heaven, he reaches out to take us by the hand, saying, "Come with me, it is time to go."

Hand-placer

The gracious hand of our God is on everyone who looks to him, but his great anger is against all who forsake him ... the hand of our God was on us, and he protected us from enemies and bandits along the way.

—Ezra 8:22b, 31b

- Ezra proclaimed a fast so the people could appeal to God for protection from attack on the long, dangerous journey from Persia to Jerusalem.
- God can protect his people from all kinds of dangers, including bandits (or muggers today) and enemies. It is as if his giant hand is poised over us to keep us safe.
- Praise God, under whose mighty hand we live and move in safety.

Head-lifter

> But you are a shield around me, O Lord; you bestow glory on me and *lift up my head*.
>
> —Ps 3:3

- People hang their head as an expression of shame, discouragement, or of defeat.
- All three may have been part of the reason King David hung his head when he fled his palace after the coup orchestrated by Absalom, his son. David's failings as a father were partly responsible for Absalom's actions. Hanging his head as he departed Jerusalem while enduring the mocking and verbal abuse of his critics would be entirely understandable.
- But David, despite this defeat, trusted God. He cried out to him (v. 4) and thanked him for lifting his head.
- Praise God, our Head-lifter, who overcomes our shame, discouragement, and our failures by his grace, reminding us that we are loved and cherished not because of how we are doing, but because of how Jesus did on the cross.

Heart-changer

The Spirit of the Lord will come upon you in power, and you will prophesy with them; and *you will be changed into a different person* . . . As Saul turned to leave Samuel, *God changed Saul's heart*, and all these signs were fulfilled that day.

—1 Sam 10:6, 9

- Saul, Israel's first king, did not have the qualifications to be the king God desired, so God did transforming work in his life, equipping him to rule.
- We are powerless to change people who need to be changed. We are sometimes unable even to successfully change ourselves, let alone one another. It would be such a nice ability to have, but would we have the wisdom to wield it?
- God has the power to radically change people from the inside out. This doctrine of regeneration is a work of the Holy Spirit, and it takes place the moment a person chooses to become a follower of Christ, transforming them into a new creation in Christ Jesus (2 Cor 5:17).
- Praise God for his ongoing, life-changing work in us and in those we love.

Heart-former

From heaven the Lord looks down and sees all humankind; from his dwelling place he watches all who live on earth—he who *forms the hearts of all*, who considers everything they do.

—Ps 33:13–15

- God is the creator of all things, including all people, here expressed in terms of forming our hearts.
- Picture God lovingly forming and making your life, much as a potter forms a vase, marking it with every pleasing detail.
- Praise God today that we were lovingly and purposefully knit together in our mothers' wombs by God so that we might know and love him and be known and loved by him.

Heart-hardener

For it was the Lord himself who *hardened their hearts* to wage war against Israel, so that he might destroy them totally, exterminating them without mercy, as the Lord had commanded Moses.

—JOSH 11:20

- God determined that he was going to judge the nations of Canaan for their wickedness, which included the sins of child sacrifice and idolatry. The means he would use was war. The Canaanites hated God and his people, Israel, so he chose to harden their hearts. They had poured the cement of their wickedness out against God, so he chose to harden it.
- God is a heart-changer. He can show grace and soften hard hearts so they will warm toward him. But he can also choose to further harden already-hard hearts, affirming the people's choice. This is a sobering warning to those who persist in their sins. God's judgment may begin before death by his confirming and accepting the bent of the wayward heart.
- Praise God for his mercy and for his willingness to forgive his enemies, if they will repent, and call them friends. Praise him too for his justice in dealing with those who will not repent but instead persist in defying him.

Heart-holder

The king's heart is in the hand of the Lord; he directs it like a watercourse wherever he pleases.

—Prov 21:1

- There is a tension in the Bible between God's sovereignty and human responsibility in decision-making. This side of heaven is a mystery beyond our ability to fully comprehend.
- God can work and move in the king's heart in such a way that the king will choose, without coercion, exactly what God wants him to do.
- Praise God that he is master over the hearts and minds of all people and can direct them as he pleases. Praise him for his presence in the Holy Spirit, who guides and directs our hearts so that we are prompted to choose what it is that God desires.

Heart-looker

The Lord does not look at the things man looks at. Man looks at the outward appearance, but the Lord looks at the heart.

—1 Sam 16:7b

- When a man was to be chosen to replace King Saul, Samuel bypassed the bigger, stronger, and taller sons of Jesse to choose the kid brother, David. God was more interested in the heart than in outward appearances or physical prowess. The man David replaced was head and shoulders above his peers, but he was a disappointment to God.
- Reflect on the truth that God cares more about the state of our hearts than he does about the attributes of our bodies. Our outer selves may be unimpressive or flawed, but our inner selves will live on, growing stronger and becoming more like Christ.
- Praise God for his attention to our inner person.

Heart-mover

In the first year of Cyrus, King of Persia, in order to fulfill the word of the Lord spoken to Jeremiah, *the Lord moved the heart of Cyrus*, King of Persia, to make a proclamation through his realm and to put it in writing.

—2 Chr 36:22

- This is an amazing thing. King Cyrus may have been the most powerful man in the world in his day. Yet the Lord moved this man's heart as easily as a child moves toy blocks across the floor.
- When God chooses to move a person's heart for his purposes, no one is able to prevent it. What an amazing ability and what an amazing God!
- Praise God for is power to work and move inside people who need a change of heart. Praise God for his ability to work in our hearts and in those we love who have closed off their hearts. God has access there and can do his work.

Heart-opener

One of those listening was a woman named Lydia, a dealer in purple cloth from the city of Thyatira, who was a worshiper of God. *The Lord opened her heart* to respond to Paul's message.

—Acts 16:14

- While Paul preached the gospel message to a group of people in Philippi, including Lydia, Luke noted that her response was the result of God's work in her heart.
- God opens the hearts of people who are not Christians, prompting them to choose to turn to God in repentance and have faith in the Lord, Jesus Christ.
- Praise God for his mysterious, supernatural work in our lives. Let us pray for him to do the same in those we know and love who need Christ.

Heart-toucher

Saul also went to his home in Gibeah, accompanied by valiant men *whose hearts God had touched.*

—1 Sam 10:26

- When Saul was made king of Israel, the nation was militarily weak, and many were skeptical as to whether he would be able to do much as king. But God touched the hearts of a number of valiant men so that they felt a desire to ally themselves with the new king and serve in his military.
- God has the ability to reach out a finger and touch people's hearts, causing them to want to do what God wants them to do.
- Wouldn't it be nice to be able to reach into people's hearts and touch them, causing them to be kinder, nicer, or more patient? None but the One has that kind of power.
- Praise God, the heart-toucher, who works in a quiet, unseen way to move people to do what he wants.

Heart-turner and Director

Turn my heart toward your statutes and not toward selfish gain.
—Ps 119:36

May the Lord *direct your hearts* into God's love and Christ's perseverance.
—2 Thess 3:5

- Just as a steering wheel turns a car where the driver wants, God is able to turn the human heart exactly as he wishes.
- Why don't we direct our own hearts toward God's statutes or into God's love and perseverance? Frankly, because often we cannot, and too often, we are not motivated to follow through. Just as we need God to do the saving and regenerating work within us for salvation, so we are dependent on God to direct our hearts toward what is right and good.
- Praise God for his ability to turn our hearts to direct them in the way they should go.

Helper

God is our refuge and strength, *an ever-present help* in trouble. Therefore we will not fear, though the earth give way and the mountains fall into the heart of the sea.

—Ps 46:1–2

The Lord is with me; I will not be afraid. What can man do to me? The Lord is with me; *he is my helper.* I will look in triumph on my enemies.

—Ps 118:6–7

Because he himself suffered when he was tempted, he is *able to help* those who are being tempted.

—Heb 2:18

- We all need help from time to time.
- There are some careers that are actually called "the helping professions," like careers with the police, firefighting, nursing, counseling, etc.
- God is our helper. Our need for help can take many forms—rescue from peril, encouragement, power to resist temptation, overcoming fear, and more.
- Praise God that he is ever-present and will help us as we call out to him in faith. His help may not come instantly (though at times it

does), but rest assured that he will help. Other times, he delays his help so he can accomplish some other work in us, like building our faith, or developing our patience, or exposing wrong attitudes in us that need addressing.

Hemmer

You *hem* me in—behind and before; you have laid your hand upon me.

—Ps 139:5

- Tailors hem up the edges of garments so that the edge of the material will not fray, unravel, or be pulled apart.
- Similarly, God hems us in so that we don't come apart under the stresses of life. He protects us from being pulled apart.
- Farmers and shepherds hem in their animals at night in enclosures so they can be kept safe from predators.
- God's enclosure gives us peace.
- Praise God for safely hemming us in, especially in a world that is fraying at the edges.

Holy

> Exalt the Lord our God and worship at his holy mountain,
> for *the Lord our God is holy.*
>
> —Ps 99:9

- Sin has tainted everything in the world. There are many beautiful things and nice people, but even so, they all bear the marks of a fallen world.
- But God is sinless and pure, untainted by sin. He is like no one and nothing we have ever seen. When Isaiah peeked behind heaven's curtain in Isa 6, he saw angels who called back and forth to each other, saying, "Holy, holy, holy is the Lord Almighty; the whole earth is full of his glory" (6:3). These angels covered their eyes with their wings to shield them from the radiating glory of God's nature.
- Praise God for his sinless nature and for the world to come, where sin will be banished and we shall all be made holy, even as he is holy.
- Praise him for his plan to remove all the ugliness of sin that mars his creation and his creatures, including us.

Home-blesser

The Lord's curse is on the house of the wicked,
but *he blesses the home of the righteous.*

—Prov 3:33

- This is a great verse to read whenever a Christian moves into a new home or apartment.
- God honors and blesses those who honor him. This verse is a statement of fact: God blesses the homes of people who, like Joshua, say, "But as for me and my household, we will serve the Lord" (Josh 24:15b).
- Praise God that he blesses our homes and all the righteous who live there.

Honorer

Whoever serves me must follow me; and where I am, my servant also will be. My *Father will honor* the one who serves me.

—JOHN 12:26

- God the Father so loves Jesus, God the Son, that our Father promises to honor every person who serves and follows Jesus.
- It seems backwards somehow that we are honored when it is obviously God who is most deserving of honor and glory. Yet God will honor us. How? The Bible speaks of our being seated with Christ in the heavenly realms and of our judging nations. It is likely much more than that. One more surprise to look forward to in heaven!
- Praise God for his willingness to honor fallen and flawed (and forgiven!) people like us. He is generous with his blessings.

Hope-giver

Remember your word to your servant, for *you have given me hope.*

—Ps 119:49

- Hope in the Bible is more than wishful thinking; it is a deep and settled conviction that what God has promised is fact and will certainly come to pass.
- God has made an untold number of promises to Christians, both for this life and for the life to come. Despite present suffering, loss, sorrow, and pain, we will one day leave all such things behind and enter into the presence of the Lord, where there is joy forevermore.
- Praise God for the blessed hope we have in Christ Jesus (Titus 2:13–14). Through him, we have forgiveness, eternal life, heaven, a joy-filled eternity, God's daily presence, and God's help in times of need.

House-builder

I declare to you that the Lord will build a house for you.

—1 Chr 17:10b

Unless *the Lord builds the house*, its builders labor in vain.

—Ps 127:1a

- King David wanted to build a house for God—a permanent temple in Jerusalem to replace the portable tabernacle. God told him that he was not the one to build such a temple, but rather his son Solomon would do it. Then God told David that God would build him a house. This would not be a physical building, but rather a line of descendants that would extend down through time and into eternity. David's "house" would culminate in Jesus, the son of David and Savior of the world.
- Christians naturally want to do something great for God. We are able to serve him in many ways. But God wants to do something for us as well, to build us a heritage that spans time into eternity. We join his spiritual family, becoming sons and daughters of God who will one day live with him in a house prepared for us.
- Praise Jesus, who told us that his Father has a big house with room for us all and that when our work on earth is done, he will bring us there to live with him: "In my Father's house are many rooms . . . and if I go and prepare a place for you, I will come back and take you to be with me that you also may be where I am" (John 14:2–3).

Humbler

Remember how the Lord your God led you all the way in the desert these forty years, to humble you and to test you in order to know what was in your heart, whether or not you would keep his commands.

—Deut 8:2

- Due to their disobedience to God's command to enter the promised land, God disciplined the nation of Israel by causing them to wander in the wilderness for forty years. Many lessons were learned in this forty-year exercise, including the lessons of humility and dependence on God.
- Pride is the opposite of humility, and it is a sin that harms us and offends God. Out of his great love for us, God exposes our pride and then works with us to remove it.
- If we will not humble ourselves under God's mighty hand so that he may lift us up, then God will humble us. He uses his unlimited power and wisdom to do so by placing us in situations beyond our resources so that our need for God becomes obvious.
- Praise God for his determination to protect us from pride's poisonous fruit by humbling us.

Hurler

Even though someone is pursuing you to take your life, the life of my master will be bound securely in the bundle of the living by the Lord your God. But the lives of your enemies *he will hurl away* as from the pocket of a sling.

—1 Sam 25:29

- These words of Abigail, wife of the fool Nabal, are directed at David, who is on the run from King Saul. She speaks eloquently of her confidence that God will protect David, for his life is "bound securely in the bundle of the living." She is equally confident that God will toss David's enemies into the next county, so to speak.

- God can hurl away anyone he chooses. There are many Sauls in the world today: people of power and violence who seek to keep their power by any means. God will deal with all such people in his time, either now or in eternity, where they shall be hurled into the pit of hell.

- When we see the wicked prosper in this world, we should praise God for his justice, which will cause him to hurl them from his presence. Praise him too that he is able to securely tie our lives and those of our loved ones in the bundle of living.

Husband

For your Maker is your *husband*—the Lord Almighty is his name—the Holy One of Israel is your Redeemer; he is called the God of all the earth.

—Isa 54:5

- Unfaithful nation Israel is compared by God to an abandoned, deserted, childless, and desolate wife (Isa 54:1–10).
- God then describes himself as Israel's devoted husband who promises to bless her and to once again relate to her "with deep compassion" (v. 7), "everlasting kindness" (v. 8), and "unfailing love." Never again will he be angry with her (v. 9). How gracious!
- The Apostle Paul uses this same husband imagery for God when he urges husbands to love their wives in the same way that God in Christ Jesus loved his people, "Husbands, love your wives, just as Christ loved the church and gave himself up for her. . . In this same way, husbands ought to love their wives, . . ." (Eph 5:25, 28).
- Consider this marvelous husband-imagery that God uses to express his love and devotion to us. He compares himself to a husband who is so deeply in love with his wife that he is willing to do whatever is needed to bless and provide for her, even to the point of laying down his life for her.
- What great love! What a great God, who, despite our sin and unfaithfulness, found a way through the cross to redeem and restore us in a lasting love-relationship.

Impartial

For the Lord your God is God of gods and Lord of lords, the great God, mighty and awesome, who *shows no partiality* and accepts no bribes.

—Deut 10:17

- Too often in this world, who you know can be more important that what you know. It is frustrating to be passed over for a job because a less qualified person is a favorite of the boss.
- With God, there is no favoritism. There are no big people and no little people. Just people. No one has an inside track with him to lobby for his favor and benefits. God is just and has no favorites.
- Praise God for his incorruptibility. He cannot be influenced to act in any manner other than what is just, fair, and right.

Jealous

For the Lord your God is a consuming fire, *a jealous God.*

—Deut 4:24

- Some think of jealousy as a weakness or an expression of insecurity. But jealousy can be a positive character trait. If we see a married woman ignore another woman who is kissing her husband, what is our opinion of her? Negative, I hope. She should march right over and deal with the situation (and with her husband!) and put an end to this inappropriate behavior. She is justified in not wanting to share her husband with anyone else.

- The Bible uses the marriage relationship to describe the kind of covenant bond that exists between God and his children. And because God loves us, he will not put up with any hint of unfaithfulness on our part.

- Praise God for his holy jealousy, which causes him to aggressively confront any threat to our relationship.

Joy

Then will I go to the altar of God, to God, *my joy*, and my delight.

—Ps 43:4

- The psalmist is longing for God's deliverance so that he can go to the temple and spend time enjoying God in worship.
- God created the world to be a place of pleasure and enjoyment for us. King Solomon said, "So I commend the enjoyment of life, because nothing is better for a man under the sun than to eat and drink and be glad. Then *joy* will accompany him in his work all the days of the life God has given him under the sun" (Eccl 8:15).
- Our greatest joy, however, is not derived from God's gifts but from God himself, the greatest of gifts.

Joyful

At that time Jesus, *full of joy* through the Holy Spirit, said, "I praise you, Father, Lord of heaven and earth, because you have hidden these things from the wise and learned, and revealed them to little children. Yes, Father, for this was your good pleasure."

—Luke 10:21

- When the seventy-two disciples returned from their mission trip to report to Jesus of their great success, Jesus was thrilled and "full of joy."
- God is the most joy-filled being in the universe. He is neither somber nor grumpy but rather joyful. Jesus told his disciples, "I have told you this so that *my joy* may be in you and that your joy may be complete" (John 15:11).
- As you reflect on God, who does all his work with a joyful enthusiasm, praise him that he is not as some religions portray him—vindictive, moody, and unpredictable—but rather is overflowing with joy.

Joy-giver

You became imitators of us and of the Lord; in spite of severe suffering, you welcomed the message with the *joy given by the Holy Spirit*.

—1 Thess 1:6

- How great would it be to be able to cheer up people who are discouraged, suffering, or despondent? In reality, our efforts meet with limited success.
- But God can give joy today just as he did to this new church. In spite of severe suffering, the Thessalonian Christians joyfully embraced the gospel message. Joy and suffering are not mutually exclusive. God can give joy to us even while we are undergoing great suffering, as Paul testified: "sorrowful, yet always rejoicing" (2 Cor 6:10).
- Praise God for his ability to give joy to the human heart regardless of circumstances.

Judge

Let the heavens rejoice, let the earth be glad; let the sea resound, and all that is in it; let the fields be jubilant, and everything in them. Then all the trees of the forest will sing for joy; they will sing before the Lord for he comes, *he comes to judge the earth*. He will judge the world in righteousness and the peoples in his truth.

—Ps 96:11–13

- Too many people live in places where the judicial system is corrupted by greed and selfishness. There is a deep longing in the human heart for wrongs to be righted with justice.
- Here the psalmist speaks of all creation rejoicing and celebrating because God comes to judge the earth. Judgment is not a negative thing; it is a positive, celebratory act. All creation recognizes the need for a just Judge to address the injustices in the world.
- Join with all creation in praising God for his justice. Reflect on how different our world would be if there was no crime and all people were honest and just.
- Praise God that our Judge has declared us "not guilty" because Jesus was a worthy substitute and took the judgment of our sins upon himself on the cross.

Just

> He is the Rock, his works are perfect, and all his ways are *just*. A faithful God who does no wrong, upright and *just* is he.
>
> —Deut 32:4

- In courtrooms around the world, people wait expectantly for justice to be administered by a man or woman who they hope is blind to all but the truth.
- Praise God that he is not merely a Judge, but that he is a Judge who is just in all his dealings, doing no wrong.
- Praise God for Jesus, whose voluntary death on the cross in our place satisfied the demands of justice, allowing guilty sinners to be pardoned: "God presented him as a sacrifice of atonement, through faith in his blood. He did this to demonstrate his *justice*, because in his forbearance he had left the sins committed beforehand unpunished—he did it to demonstrate his *justice* at the present time, so as to be *just* and the one who *justifies* those who have faith in Jesus" (Rom 3:25–26).

Justice-granter

> And will not God *bring about justice* for his chosen ones, who cry out to him day and night? Will he keep putting them off? I tell you, he will see that they get justice, and quickly.
>
> —Luke 18:7–8a

- Jesus told of a woman who persistently appealed her case to a disinterested judge. The judge finally rendered his verdict just to get rid of her. Jesus contrasted that corrupt judge against God, who does not need to be badgered by his chosen ones before he will pay attention to their needs.

- We have God's promise that he will see to it that we get justice, and quickly. We know by experience and through other Scriptures that God may also choose to delay his judgment for various reasons, including giving the unjust more time to repent (2 Pet 3:8–9).

- Praise God that any injustices we have endured in the past or are enduring today will be rectified as we, in faith, call out to him for justice.

Justice-lover

The King is mighty, *he loves justice*—you have established equity. In Jacob you have done what is just and right.

—Ps 99:4

- It is possible for judges to see their profession as just a job, a way to make a living. And there would be nothing wrong with that, I suppose. However, how much better would it be if every judge had a burning passion to see justice done and rejoiced at heart whenever it prevailed?
- God is not only just—he loves justice. His mind and his heart are fully engaged in its pursuit.
- Praise God that he is a lover of justice. He has a passion to see that every person who is abused, exploited, or oppressed receives just treatment.

Justifier

But the tax collector stood at a distance. He would not even look up to heaven, but beat his breast and said, "God, have mercy on me, a sinner." I tell you that this man, rather than the other, went home *justified before God.* For everyone who exalts himself will be humbled, and he who humbles himself will be exalted.

—Luke 18:13–14

- Two men went to the temple to pray. One man was confident of his own righteousness and looked down on everybody else. The other was a hated tax collector. Surprisingly, it was the tax collector who earned God's favor, not the religious man with his résumé full of good works.
- God justifies people, but only when they admit their spiritual poverty and throw themselves on the mercy of God for forgiveness and acceptance.
- Praise God that he is not only just, he is also the One who justifies sinners. He forgives our sin and credits righteousness to us, "the righteousness that comes from God and is by faith" (Phil 3:9). Reflect and rejoice in the fact that our mountain of sins has been removed and that when God looks at us, it is as if we had not committed those sins.

Keeper

The Lord will *keep you* from all harm—he will watch over your life.

—Ps 121:7

And this is the will of him who sent me, that I *shall lose none* of all that he has given me, but raise them up at the last day.

—John 6:39

- We keep our valuables in a safe place so they are not stolen or lost.
- God is also capable of keeping his valuables safe. He is able to shield and safeguard what is valuable to him—namely, us! God the Father has given his elect to God the Son, and Jesus declared that he would not lose a single one of those entrusted into his care and keeping.
- Praise God that you are kept by him and thus need not fear or despair. God will keep you safe in this world as he deems best in your personalized discipleship program, and he will keep your soul safe: "because I know whom I have believed, and am convinced that he is able to guard what I have entrusted to him for that day" (2 Tim 1:12).

Key-holder

I am the Living One; I was dead, and behold I am alive for ever and ever! And *I hold the keys* of death and Hades.

—Rev 1:18

- Keys grant access, authority, and power. If you have keys to a building or a car, you have access to it, authority to enter, and the power to use it for your purposes.

- Jesus, by virtue of his death and resurrection, has been granted the keys to death and Hades, the place of the dead. He can unlock the door to death, enter, and take back whomever he wants—death no longer has power or authority over those who die. Wherever the dead go, Jesus now has control of that domain.

- Praise God that Christians have no need to fear death or what lies beyond it, because Jesus has defeated death by his resurrection and claimed authority over death's domain. We have nothing to fear from death. Jesus removed its sting and its ability to terrorize us: "'Where, O death, is your victory? Where, O death, is your sting?' The sting of death is sin, and the power of sin is the law. But thanks be to God! He gives us the victory through our Lord Jesus Christ" (1 Cor 15:55–57).

Killer

He struck down many nations and killed *mighty kings—Sihon, king of the Amorites, Og, king of Bashan, and all the kings of Canaan—and he gave their land as an inheritance, an inheritance to his people, Israel.*

—Ps 135:10–12

- From the time of Adam and Eve's fall into sin in Eden, God has decreed that death shall fall upon all humankind. Whenever anyone dies, it is a direct result of the introduction of sin into the world and God's judgment against it. How and when death occurs is determined by God. Here, God determines the time and the means of the deaths of the kings of Canaan and the wicked peoples who populated the land.

- Praise be to God that even though we will physically die as a result of our sin, our death has been absorbed by Jesus on the cross, so that it has lost all its power and thus its terror. As Jesus said, "I tell you the truth, if anyone keeps my word, he will never see death" (John 8:51). And again, "I tell you the truth, whoever hears my word and believes him who sent me has eternal life and will not be condemned; he has crossed over from death to life" (John 5:24).

- Rejoice in Jesus, who allowed himself to be killed so that we would be spared.

King

You are my *King* and my God, who decrees victories for Jacob.

—Ps 44:4

- A king has a kingdom, subjects, authority, power, and the adoration of his subjects.
- Whereas some royal families suffer from embarrassing episodes involving family members, God is always worthy of our admiration.
- Upon his return to earth, Jesus will be acknowledged as the "King of kings and Lord of lords" (Rev 19:16b).
- Whereas a king should come forth with pomp and majesty, the Lord Jesus did what no king ever had—he laid aside his royal privileges, suffered abuse at the hands of his subjects, and died for them.
- Praise God that we are the subjects of such a kind and good King.

King-crusher

The Lord is at your right hand; *he will crush kings* on the day of his wrath. He will judge the nations, heaping up the dead and *crushing the rulers* of the whole earth.

—Ps 110:5–6

- Although it is not so today, monarchs in biblical days generally ruled with unquestioned power and authority. They could—and did—crush any who challenged, displeased, or opposed them.
- God is the greatest of all kings. He rules justly and has the power to crush those who, in their wickedness, oppose him or his people. Using the imagery and language of contemporary warfare, this psalm describes the day when God will reclaim his full right to reign over his creation, crushing all who defy him.
- "Then the kings of the earth, the princes, the generals, the rich, the mighty, and every slave and every free man hid in caves and among the rocks of the mountains. They called to the mountains and the rocks, 'Fall on us and hide us from the face of him who sits on the throne and from the wrath of the Lamb! For the great day of their wrath has come, and who can stand?" (Rev 6:15–17).
- Praise God that no human king or president will be able to defiantly stand before the God of justice and righteousness when he comes to make all things right through his Son, Jesus.

Knitter

For you created my inmost being; *you knit me* together in my mother's womb . . . My frame was not hidden from you when I was made in the secret place. When *I was woven* together in the depths of the earth, your eyes saw my unformed body.

—Ps 139:13, 15–16A

- Knitters take skeins of yarn and bind them together into mittens or sweaters. Balls of yarn are transformed into useful articles of clothing.
- When we are conceived and begin life's journey in our mothers' wombs, God, in some marvelous and mysterious way, knits us together. Even though he does not use needles and yarn, still we are his handiwork and have worth because we are his handiwork.
- Praise God for silently knitting us together in our mothers' wombs. We are not accidents of nature but are "fearfully and wonderfully made" (v. 14).

Lamb of God

> The next day John saw Jesus coming toward him and said, "Look, the *Lamb of God*, who takes away the sin of the world!"
>
> —JOHN 1:29

- Only here and in John 1:36 is the expression "the Lamb of God" used to describe our Lord (although he is referred to as the Lamb elsewhere in the New Testament). This term used for Jesus harkens back to the Passover celebration in Egypt, where the Angel of Death passed over the homes of those who smeared their doorposts with the blood of a lamb. Innocent and helpless, the spilled blood of these lambs covered the sins of their owners.
- Praise God for Jesus, who volunteered to come to earth and the cross to be "led like a lamb to the slaughter" (Isa 53:7b) so that we might be reconciled to God.

Lamp

You are *my lamp*, O Lord; the Lord turns my darkness into light.

—2 Sam 22:29

- When the power goes out in the night, a flashlight or a lamp is highly valued.
- In life, God functions as a light, giving us the ability to see our way to safety.
- After God delivered King David from his enemies (especially King Saul), he sang this song. In it, he calls God his lamp, shining light on his path so that he can walk in safety.
- Praise God that in our literal and figurative times of darkness, his word and presence can be our lamp, lighting our way.
- "The Lord is my light and salvation—whom shall I fear?" (Ps 27:1).

Lamp-bearer

The lamp of the Lord searches the spirit of a man;
it searches out his inmost being.

—Prov 20:27

- Thankfully, flashlights have replaced oil lamps as tools to aid us in the dark.
- God searches inside people as easily as we shine a flashlight in the back of a closet when we are searching for a misplaced item.
- Jeremiah notes that the human heart is a twisted, unfixable maze of deceit. He then notes that while we cannot untangle the heart's web, God can. He said, "The heart is deceitful above all things and beyond cure. Who can understand it?" He then answers his own question: "I the Lord search the heart and examine the mind, to reward a man according to his conduct, according to what his deeds deserve" (Jer 17:9–10).
- Praise God that he knows our hearts and shines his light in the darkest corners to identify and remove anything that is harmful to us or offensive to him. Praise him too that he rewards us according to what he finds in our hearts.

Law-abolisher

By abolishing in his flesh *the law* with its commandments and regulations. His purpose was to create in himself one new man out of the two, thus making peace.

—Eph 2:15

- The context of Eph 2 addresses the Old Testament separation of the Jews, as God's covenant people, from the Gentiles, who were outside that covenant. Gentiles were "excluded from citizenship in Israel and foreigners to the covenants of the promise, without hope and without God in the world" (v. 12). But now that covenant, with its "commandments and regulations," has been revised and expanded by Jesus and his atoning work to incorporate both Jews and Gentiles into "one new man" (v. 15).
- Jesus came to fulfill the Law, but he also came to reveal a new way "and be found in him, not having a righteousness of my own that comes from the law, but that which is through faith in Christ Jesus—the righteousness that comes from God and is by faith" (Phil 3:9).
- Praise God that the Lord Jesus has removed all barriers to God, allowing all the peoples of the world to have equal access to God through Jesus. We don't have to be Jewish or follow the Old Testament Jewish commandments and regulations in order to have access to God.

Leader

Teach me to do your will, for you are my God;
may your good Spirit *lead me on level ground.*

—Ps 143:10

- When we find ourselves lost in a maze of corridors or in a tangle of paths in the forest, it is so nice to have someone say, "I know the way. Follow me."
- God leads people who are willing to trust and follow him. He leads us through the words of the Bible that he has graciously provided for us. He leads through circumstances, through the wise advice of others, and through his Spirit's still, small voice, which speaks to us when we tune our hearing to his voice.
- Praise God that he is a leading God who puts our feet on level ground so that we do not stumble.

Leaver

But when envoys were sent by the rulers of Babylon to ask him about the miraculous sign that had occurred in the land, *God left him* to test him and to know everything that was in his heart.

—2 Chr 32:31

- King Hezekiah did a foolish thing when he invited representatives of a foreign government to tour his treasuries. It was a decision he lived to regret.
- God withdrew for a time to observe his servant. Hezekiah promptly failed the test.
- Jesus promised to never leave us. This comforting truth does not, however, prevent us from occasionally losing our sense of the closeness of God. When this happens, it is not a punishment but a test of our faith.
- Praise God that in his love for us, he wisely uses a variety of means to grow and transform us, including occasionally leaving us without a sense of his closeness.

Life

This day I call heaven and earth as witnesses against you that I have set before you life and death, blessings and curses. Now choose life, so that you and your children may live and that you may love the Lord your God, listen to his voice, and hold fast to him. For *the Lord is your life*, and he will give you many years in the land he swore to give to your fathers, Abraham, Isaac, and Jacob.

—Deut 30:19–20

- As the nation of Israel stood on the boundary of the promised land, waiting to enter and lay claim to the inheritance God was offering them, they were admonished to love God, listen to him, and hold fast to him. Why? Because he was their life.
- Sometimes people in despair say that life is not worth living. They have lost something—or more often, someone—that they believe they cannot live without.
- God is our life. Without him, life is not worth living. With him, our lives become lives of hope, blessing, and promise. They will not necessarily be lives free of heartache or trouble, but the blessings of God will overshadow all suffering and loss.
- Praise God that he alone makes life worth living. Regardless of what we lose (health, money, independence, loved ones, etc.), we gain far, far more in Christ.

Life-giver

> And he is not served by human hands, as if he needed anything, because he himself *gives all men life* and breath and everything else.
>
> —Acts 17:25

- The people of Athens considered themselves experts on all things religious. However, when Paul arrived in the city and began to teach about Jesus and the resurrection, these experts were baffled. In response to their invitation, Paul preached about Jesus. Part of his message was a call to consider the God who is powerful enough to give life to every human being on the planet.
- Rarely do we consider the marvel and mystery of life. Like the first-opened Christmas present, the gift of life is soon forgotten as our attention is directed toward other unopened gifts.
- In one sense we are given life by our parents, but in the ultimate sense we are given life by God, who uses our parents as his agents to bring us into existence. Thus, we owe him everything.
- Imagine being able to create life. What a power! And God continues to display his power in our lives by giving us *everything else* we need.
- Praise God for life—yours, the lives of those you love, and of all living things. Praise to the One who is the Life-giver.

Life-holder

But you did not honor the God who *holds in his hand your life* and all your ways.

—Dan 5:23b

- King Belshazzar of Babylon, carried away with his own greatness, defied God, and in so doing, made a fatal miscalculation. He failed to take into account that his life and his kingdom fit neatly into the palm of God's hand. At any time, God could flick him away as easily as we brush a crumb from the table. Daniel delivered the message: "That very night Belshazzar, king of the Babylonians, was slain" (v. 30).
- God's hand is so big that all of us easily fit inside, living out our lives under his watchful gaze. Quite a picture!
- Praise the One in whose mighty hand we are safely ensconced. We have nothing to fear.
- Jesus said, "I give them eternal life, and they shall never perish; no one can snatch them out of my hand. My Father, who has given them to me, is greater than all; no one can snatch them out of my Father's hand. I and the Father are one" (John 10:28–30).

Life Preserver

Preserve my life according to your love,
and I will obey the statutes of your mouth.

—Ps 119:88

- Ships carry life preservers, or as they are called now, "personal flotation devices." If passengers go overboard, these flotation devices will save their lives, keeping them afloat until rescue arrives.
- God is our life preserver. The storms of life can swamp our boats or toss us into the angry waves. However, we need not panic, because God, in his love, is with us and will preserve us.
- Praise God that no matter what we face, we will ultimately be safe because God will enable us to float above the waves of any situation.

Lifter

> But *he lifted the needy* out of their affliction and increased their families like flocks.
>
> —Ps 107:41

- The psalmist talks about God's practice of disciplining ancient Israel when the nation turned from him. He would send drought or foreign armies into the land to bring hardship, which would lead Israel to repent. Then, in his kindness, he would deliver them, lifting them out of the trouble.
- God's love is at times expressed in allowing hardship to befall his children. It can be to test or purify our faith or to expose sin in us so it can be addressed.
- After we place our faith in Christ, God's actions toward us are always governed by love. When we are afflicted, God will—in his own good time—lift us out of our hardship, giving us relief.
- Praise God that he is able and willing to lift us out of our troubles.

Light of the World

When Jesus spoke again to the people, he said, "*I am the light of the world. Whoever follows me will never walk in darkness, but will have the light of life.*"

—JOHN 8:12

- Light illuminates that which is in the dark. We know what it is to try to find our way in the dark. Even familiar rooms become dangerous obstacle courses as we bump blindly into furniture and walls. But turn on the light, and our tentative baby steps in the dark become confident strides.
- Just as physical light illuminates our path, Jesus, the light of the world, illuminates our hearts and minds, enabling us to see truth and error. By his light, we live with confidence.
- Praise God for Jesus, the light of the world, and for the Holy Spirit, who shines the words of Jesus on our path so we know how to live.

Light-wrapper

Praise the Lord, O my soul. O Lord my God, you are very great; you are clothed with splendor and majesty. He wraps himself in light *as with a garment; he stretches out the heavens like a tent.*

—Ps 104:1–2

- The imagery here is of the Lord putting on splendor, majesty, and light just as we put on clothes.
- The aura surrounding God in his heavenly dwelling is so glorious that humankind cannot even approach it—he "lives in unapproachable light" (1 Tim 6:16).
- Reflect on the great glory of God in heaven, surrounded by countless angelic beings amidst a glorious brilliance that rivals the light of the sun.
- Praise Jesus, whose human form masked his divine glory, except for that brief moment on the Mount of Transfiguration when Luke said, "the appearance of his face changed, and his clothes became as bright as a flash of lightning" (Luke 9:29). One day we shall see him in all his radiant brilliance and marvel.

Longing God

I *long to redeem them*, but they speak lies against me. They do not cry out to me from their hearts but wail upon their beds. They gather together for grain and new wine but turn away from me.

—Hos 7:13b–14

- God entered into a loving covenant relationship with his people, Israel, but they regularly turned their backs to him and worshiped other gods. They gathered with their friends, but they had no desire to gather with God—they turned away from him.
- We understand the longings of the human heart, whether for a prodigal child to return or to find that one special person to share our life with.
- God's heart is full of longing as well. He longs to redeem and reconcile his prodigal children, but they will not turn to him. As in the days of Noah, God's heart is pained and grieved over the sins of his children (Gen 6:6).
- Praise our longing God for his tender heart and for his ardent desire to redeem lost people.

Looker on the Lowly

Though the Lord is on high, *he looks upon the lowly*,
but the proud he knows from afar.

—Ps 138:6

- The famous, important, and powerful people of the world rarely have the time or interest to notice the average person.
- No one is more famous, important, or powerful than God, and yet he takes note of and cares for those who are weak, small, and lowly.
- God said, "I live in a high and holy place, but also with him who is contrite and lowly in spirit, to revive the spirit of the lowly and to revive the heart of the contrite" (Isa 57:15b).
- Praise God that he loves and cares for all people, but especially for those who are humble and lowly in spirit.

Lopper

See, the Lord, the Lord Almighty, *will lop off* the boughs with great power. The lofty trees will be felled, the tall ones will be brought low. He will cut down the forest thickets with an ax; Lebanon will fall before the Mighty One. A shoot will come up from the stump of Jesse; from his roots a Branch will bear fruit.

—Isa 10:33–11:1

- Before the introduction of mechanization, the harvesting of wood was done with saws and axes. Trees would be felled with saws, and then men would go over the fallen tree swinging a heavy ax, lopping off branches until the trunk was bereft of all limbs.
- This is the image Isaiah uses to describe what God will do to the mighty Assyrian military machine that runs rampant over Israel. Surely Assyria defeated and oppressed Israel at God's behest, but once they finished their God-ordained mission, God would humble them for their prideful arrogance. They would literally be cut down to size.
- There is no shortage of prideful and arrogant people in the world today. Praise God that the wicked, whether great or small, will feel the bite of the divine Lumberjack's ax when he restores justice and righteousness to the earth.
- Reflect on the promise of Jesus, who in Bethlehem appeared as a simple shoot rising from the stump of King David (the son of Jesse), but who will, upon his second coming, fill the entire earth.

Lord

You know the message God sent to the people of Israel, telling the good news of peace through Jesus Christ, who is *Lord of all*.

—ACTS 10:36

- The term "Lord" is not commonly used today, so we are at risk of losing its meaning. "Lord" signifies master, leader, boss, or the one in charge.
- In Peter's sermon at the home of the Gentile Cornelius, Peter stated that Jesus is "Lord of all," meaning Lord of both Jews and Gentiles, accepting "men from every nation who fear him and do what is right" (v. 35).
- Not all of us acknowledge that Jesus is the leader of all, but one day everyone will either freely or grudgingly acknowledge it, for "at the name of Jesus every knee should bow, in heaven and on earth and under the earth, and every tongue confess that Jesus is Lord, to the glory of God the Father" (Phil 2:10–11).
- Praise God for Jesus, who is our Savior and our Lord. Rejoice for the coming day when he will receive his due from all people.

Lord of Lords

For the Lord your God is God of gods and *Lord of lords*, the great God, mighty and awesome, who shows no partiality and accepts no bribes.

—Deut 10:17

- Of all the gods people have worshiped since the dawn of time, one stands apart. The Lord God declared himself superior to every entity that competes for the devotion of the human heart. He has no peer or equal. He alone is God.

- Praise God that of all the world religions with their gods, there is One who towers above all. And he is just, righteous, compassionate, loving, and good in addition to being all-powerful.

- Praise him too for Jesus, he who "hands over the kingdom to God the Father after he has destroyed all dominion, authority, and power. For he must reign until he has put all his enemies under his feet. The last enemy to be destroyed is death" (1 Cor 15:24b–26).

Love-abounder

You are forgiving and good, O Lord, *abounding in love* to all who call to you.

—Ps 86:5

- The word "abound" comes from a Latin word meaning "to overflow."
- God's love for those who call out to him in faith is said to be so abundant that it spills over. Picture a river that has spilled over its banks in springtime.
- The source of this love is said by the disciple John to be the very heart of God, whom he described as "God is love" (1 John 4:8b).
- God's love is wonderful, and the image here is of a love that overflows and spills over those to whom it is directed. For those who call out to God in faith and trust, God's love is abundant and endless.
- Praise God for his great love, so perfectly displayed by sending his Son, Jesus, into the world to reconcile us to himself.

Lover

For *God so loved the world* that he gave his one and only Son, that whoever believes in him shall not perish but have eternal life.

—John 3:16

For as high as the heavens are above the earth, *so great is his love* for those who fear him.

—Ps 103:11

- Some people are easier to love than others. We have no trouble thinking of people we love. And we can likely bring to mind some that we don't love. We tolerate some people without actually loving them. And there are others whom, in our honest moments, we confess we just don't like and don't care about.
- God loves both those who are easy to love and those who are not. He loves the worthy and the undeserving. His love is extended to all the people of the world.
- Praise God for his great love for sinful, damaged, broken, and lost people.

Majestic

The Lord reigns, he is *robed in majesty*; the Lord is *robed in majesty* and is armed with strength. The world is firmly established; it cannot be moved.

—Ps 93:1

- It seems that whenever the British royal family holds a wedding, the world stops to gaze at the splendor, pageantry, and majesty of the royals attired in all their finery.
- If we could see into heaven and gaze at God, we would marvel at how majestic and royal he looks. We would not be able to take our eyes off him.
- Applaud God for his majestic greatness. Fill your mind's eye with his splendor. Anticipate the day when we shall see him as he is (1 John 3:2).

Maker of Heaven and Earth

> May you be blessed by the Lord, the *maker of heaven and earth*.
> —Ps 115:15

- Where did the universe come from? It seems there are only three logical possibilities:
    a) It is eternal and had no beginning. Science agrees with Scripture that this cannot be.
    b) It made itself from nothing. Science again agrees with Scripture that this is not the answer.
    c) It was made.
- Although Christians disagree on exactly how the universe came into existence (e.g., young Earth vs. old Earth, or literal six days of creation or not), they do agree that God made all that exists.
- Praise God for his power to create out of nothing all that we see and all that we continue to discover, from microscopic wonders to space itself.

Maker of People

Is this the way you repay the Lord, O foolish and unwise people? Is he not your Father, your Creator, *who made you* and formed you?

—Deut 32:6

- Moses gave a farewell message to Israel in the form of a song, admonishing them to remain faithful to God after his death. He reminded them that they owed God their love and loyalty not only because of their covenant commitment, but because God created them and formed them just as surely as he did Adam from the dust of the earth.
- We know how babies are made, but it is easy to forget that the conception and development of every life is a miracle, the handiwork of God.
- Praise God that he made and formed us for his pleasure and purpose, and then, with that understanding in our heads and hearts, serve him with gladness today.

Mediator

For there is one God and one *mediator* between God and men, the man Christ Jesus, who gave himself as a ransom for all men—the testimony given in its proper time.

—1 Tim 2:5–6

- Mediators are called in to settle disputes between estranged parties.
- Because our sin offended God and alienated us from him, we need to find some way to be reconciled that will satisfy the demands of God's justice. We need a mediator.
- God provided one. God the Son would come into the world, live a sinless life as one of us, and then die in our stead. This would satisfy both the justice of God (sin was punished on the cross) and enable him to declare guilty sinners just—a remarkable and costly (to God) plan. Thus peace and reconciliation was attained.
- Praise God for Jesus, who joined our hands with the outstretched hand of God by virtue of his atoning sacrifice (Rom 3:25–26).

Memorial-giver

For this is what the Lord says: "To the eunuchs who keep my Sabbaths, who choose what pleases me and hold fast to my covenant—to them I will give within my temple and its wall a *'memorial'* and a name better than sons and daughters; I will give them an everlasting name that will not be cut off."

—Isaiah 56:4–5

- Covenant-keeping foreigners and eunuchs feared that when God restored Israel after its seventy-year exile they would not be welcomed in God's new kingdom. The foreigner thought, "Surely the Lord will exclude me from his people," (56:3) while the eunuch feared that his lack of ability to father children would disqualify him, "I am only a dry stick" (56:3).
- God reassures both the foreigner and the eunuch that he will make no distinction between them and others who are full-fledged citizens of Israel. Eunuchs, who were not permitted to enter the temple area (Deut 23:1), let alone serve in any capacity there, would in fact be honored by God with a "memorial and a name" better than sons and daughters, in the temple itself.
- The Hebrew word for "memorial" is the same word translated "monument" in 2 Sam 18:18 to describe the monument Absalom built to himself because he had no surviving sons. The Hebrew for "a memorial and a name" (*yad vashem*) was chosen as the name of the main Holocaust monument in Jerusalem in modern Israel.
- Ponder God's great love for all who "bind themselves to the Lord to serve him, to love the name of the Lord, and to worship him. . ." (56:6), regardless of disability, disadvantage, background, gender, or nation

of origin. God delights to honor those who love him with a lasting memorial and a name. Amazing!

Merciful

Who is a God like you, who pardons sin and forgives the transgression of the remnant of his inheritance? You do not stay angry forever but *delight to show mercy*. You will again have compassion on us; you will tread our sins underfoot and hurl all our iniquities into the depths of the sea.

—Mic 7:18–19

Turn to me and *have mercy* on me, as you always do to those who love your name.

—Ps 119:132

We do not make requests of you because we are righteous, but because of *your great mercy.*

—Dan 9:18b

- Mercy is the withholding of a deserved punishment or consequence.
- Humans struggle to show mercy to their enemies. Our anger tends to crowd out mercy.
- God not only shows mercy—he delights to do so. God finds joy in every opportunity he has to be merciful. If it is at all possible, he will show mercy rather than harsh judgment.
- Praise God for his merciful heart and for saving us, "not because of righteous things we have done, but because of his mercy" (Titus 3:5a).

Messiah

The woman said, "I know that *Messiah*" (called Christ) "is coming. When he comes, he will explain everything to us." Then Jesus declared, "I who speak to you am he."

—JOHN 4:25–26

- The English words "Messiah" and "Christ" come from the respective Hebrew and Greek words for "anointed one." People who were anointed were those selected or chosen for a special task (e.g., high priest or king of Israel).
- Jesus is the Anointed One, selected by God the Father to be the Savior of the world through his death on the cross and to be the Lord who will destroy all dominion, authority, and power that opposes God (1 Cor 15:24f) at the end of the age.
- Praise God for Jesus, the Anointed One, who saves us, loves us, and never leaves us.

Mighty

Who is this King of glory? The Lord strong and *mighty*, the Lord *mighty* in battle.

—Ps 24:8

- Wouldn't it be nice to have unlimited power? With unlimited financial power, you could bless others in need. With unlimited physical power, you could lift cars off injured people. With unlimited persuasive power, you could influence others to do what is right and good. Alas, our power is miniscule and limited.
- God, on the other hand, has unlimited power. He is omnipotent, meaning all-powerful. God alone has this power to do anything he chooses.
- Praise God for his unlimited power and for his commitment to use that power for good in our lives as he sees fit.

Mildew-spreader

When you enter the land of Canaan, which I am giving you as your possession, and I *put a spreading mildew* in a house in that land.

—Lev 14:34

- God stated to Israel that he may put a spreading mildew in someone's house, and if he chooses to do that, there are certain steps that need to be taken to treat it.
- God is master of all creation, including fungi. Nothing he has made is outside his control and mastery, whether it be fungus, bacteria, insects, animals, people, or planets.
- Praise God for his complete control over all things, even down to the smallest, seemingly inconsequential thing.
- What was it that Jesus said? "Are not two sparrows sold for a penny? Yet not one of them will fall to the ground apart from your Father. And even the very hairs of your head are all numbered. So don't be afraid; you are worth more than many sparrows" (Matt 10:29–31).

Mind-reader

The Lord *knows the thoughts of man*; he knows that they are futile.

—Ps 94:11

But Jesus would not entrust himself to them, for *he knew all men*. He did not need man's testimony about man, for he knew what was in a man.

—John 2:24–25

- If God offered us the power to read the minds of everyone around us, would we accept it? Despite its initial appeal, we may find it is better to not know everything others think. We may become disillusioned or offended.
- The truth is that we often don't even know our own deepest inner thoughts and motivations, let alone those of others.
- God is able to read people's minds and hearts as easily as we read words on a page.
- Praise God that he knows all our thoughts and loves us anyway. Praise him that he does not use this ability to manipulate us, but only for our good.

Mocker

He *mocks proud mockers* but gives grace to the humble.

—Prov 3:34

- Few like braggarts or those who make fun of others.
- Most people feel some satisfaction when someone who is cocky, mocking, or a braggart is put in their place. It appeals to our innate sense of justice.
- God has the ability to deal with mockers by giving them a taste of their own medicine with the goal of bringing them to change their ways so they will humbly walk before God and others.
- Praise God for his ability to effectively deal with every person according to his or her need.

Moth

I am *like a moth* to Ephraim, like rot to the people of Judah.

—Hos 5:12

- Moths and rot consume and destroy.
- God, in his judgment on Israel (Ephraim is another term for Israel), will not allow them to materially prosper as long as they live in defiance and disobedience.
- Haggai speaks of the same thing, asking people to give careful thought to the fact that although they plant much, they harvest little and that although they earn much, their money goes into a purse with holes in it (Hag 1:5–6).
- Jesus reminded us to seek first God's kingdom and his righteousness, and then God would see that our needs are provided for. To first seek anything other than God may cause the Lord to lovingly eat up what we cherish until we get our priorities right.
- Praise God for his loving chastisements, which help us return to him, the source of our joy and true blessings.

Mountain-treader

He who forms the mountains, creates the wind, and reveals his thoughts to man, he who turns dawn to darkness, and *treads the high places of the earth*—the Lord God Almighty is his name.

—Amos 4:13

- Mountain climbing is challenging exercise, but the rewards are equally satisfying—the view from the top is breathtaking. It can take hours or days to scale a mountain.
- The prophet Amos warned Israel to prepare to meet God and to give an account of their sinful ways. He stated that the God, who is big enough to stride from mountaintop to mountaintop, will surely have little trouble executing judgment on them for their sins.
- Praise God for his greatness. His footprints can be found on the highest mountain peaks of the world.

Nation-healer

Then the angel showed me the river of the water of life, as clear as crystal, flowing from the throne of God and of the Lamb down the middle of the great street of the city. On each side of the river stood the tree of life, bearing twelve crops of fruit, yielding its fruit every month. And the leaves of the tree are for *the healing of the nations.*

—Rev 22:1–3

- Listening to the news about the troubles of nations around the globe is disheartening. So many people are trapped in lands terrorized by sinful, greedy people. Humankind has made such a mess of this once-perfect world God entrusted to us.
- But praise God that one day, when history as we know it comes to an end, God will do an extreme makeover of all things, and the nations will be healed from sin's curse and from its poisoned fruit. These images from the book of Revelation are taken from Ezek 47. They fill our hearts with hope and joyous anticipation.

Nation-judger

He will judge the nations, heaping up the dead and crushing the rulers of the whole earth.

—Ps 110:6

- Millions of people are trapped in nations that persecute, imprison, and repress their own citizenry, largely beyond the help of those outsiders who want to alleviate the country's suffering. Such suffering does not escape the all-seeing eye of God.
- The Old Testament prophets spoke often of God judging the nations (including Israel), a theme that is picked up in greater detail in the book of Revelation (see 19:14–16).
- Praise God that none shall escape accountability to God for their actions. God will deal with violent people in the only terms they understand—with just and violent retribution.

Nation-watcher

He rules forever by his power, *his eyes watch the nations*—let not the rebellious rise up against him.

—Ps 66:7

- Military satellites monitor the activities of terrorists and rogue nations that are deemed a threat to world peace.
- Google satellites enable us to zoom in on any spot on Earth.
- More amazing than either of these is the fact that God keeps his eyes on the nations of the world in a way that no satellite can match.
- God has set the nations in their place (Acts 17:26), and he monitors what goes on in each. In due time, he will bring judgment against those who rise up against him.
- Praise God for his care for the nations of the world and for his vigilance in watching over all of them, doing his work in each one and bringing each to judgment in his own time.

Orphan-defender

He defends the cause of the fatherless and the widow, and loves the alien, giving him food and clothing.

—Deut 10:18

- God instituted laws for the protection of the weakest and most vulnerable in ancient Israel's society, and he gave stern warnings to those who would be tempted to exploit such people.
- God loves and cares for the orphan, the widow, and the stranger in the land, and he commands that we also seek justice and pursue it on behalf of the exploited.
- Praise God for his compassionate heart and for his love of the poor and the weak, who, in biblical days, were often the most spiritual in the land because they realized that they had no one to care for them but God.

Overcomer

I have told you these things, so that in me you may have peace. In this world you will have trouble. But take heart! *I have overcome the world!*

—John 16:33

- Who among us doesn't like a story about someone overcoming huge obstacles to succeed? There is something in us that cheers for those who succeed against great odds.
- We should cheer Jesus. Through his death, he overcame a quartet of formidable foes—sin, death, hell, and Satan. The foundation for the restoration of all things to their rightful order and Owner has been laid in Jesus' victory over death through his resurrection. Because of this victory, we have nothing to fear, now or in the future.
- "In me" is peace, said Jesus. "In this world" is trouble. We are in this world, but we are at the same time in Christ, and therefore all that he has attained is ours.
- No matter what this world brings to us by way of disappointment, heartache, loss, or pain, it is only temporary. Soon we will be with Christ, where the memories of this world will pale in comparison to the glory that will be revealed to us.
- Praise God that because Jesus has overcome the world, we can take heart and experience peace.

Owner

To the Lord your God *belong the heavens,* even the highest heavens, the *earth,* and *everything* in it.

—Deut 10:14

- Everywhere we look, we see God's "stuff." Every deed or title of ownership for property does not ultimately belong to the one whose name is listed on the document, but rather to God, who is the creator and owner of all that exists.
- God's ownership extends to all life on the planet, including human life. God owns everything.
- In his kindness, God temporarily entrusts some of his stuff to us, to care for and manage on his behalf as his stewards. One day he will require of us an accounting of how well we have managed his assets.
- Praise God, to whom we belong.

Panic-sender

Then panic struck the whole army—those in the camp and field, and those in the outposts and raiding parties—and the ground shook. It was *a panic sent by God.*

—1 Sam 14:15

- When God enabled Jonathan and his young armor-bearer to kill twenty Philistines after they sneaked into the enemy camp, God sent a ripple of panic throughout the entire army.
- Imagine the ability to send such a panic through an army of hardened military men that their courage melts away! What an amazing power!
- Praise God, who has the power to govern people's thinking and feelings. We need not fear anyone or anything, for God is with us and can overcome those who oppose us by his might or through his unseen inner workings.

Path-maker

I run in *the path of your commands*, for you have set my heart free ... Direct me in *the path of your commands*, for there I find delight.

—Ps 119:32, 35

- When walking in the woods, it is reassuring to have a path to follow. Marked trails sooth our anxiety because we know that others have gone before and marked out the way. On a path we can move quickly—even run—but without a path, we must be cautious.
- God wants us to run in life with our hearts set free.
- God's commands are like paths for us in life. If we learn them and obey them, we can move forward in safety and run freely.
- Praise God, the Path-maker, who in his love has provided us with a safe path to walk.

Path-straightener

Trust in the Lord with all your heart and lean not on you own understanding; in all your ways acknowledge him and *he will make your paths straight.*

—Prov 3:5–6

- It is said that the quickest way to get from Point A to Point B is a straight line. What is true in geometry is a bit trickier when applied to life.
- Perhaps you have experienced being lost and driving around and around while muttering, "I know it's around here somewhere." Time is wasted, and we grow frustrated at our inability to remember how to get to where we want to go.
- Life is similar. We know where we want to go, but we so often seem unable to get there. Our path is a jumbled maze.
- When we trust in God and let him lead us, our path becomes straight. With God in charge, we have a far more reliable and knowledgeable driver.
- Praise God that he can straighten our tangled paths.

Peace

For *he himself is our peace,* who has made the two one and has destroyed the barrier, the dividing wall of hostility.

—Eph 2:14

- Paul here tells us that Jesus broke down the wall of hostility that historically separated Jews from Gentiles so that both could have equal footing with God.
- Jesus is our Peacemaker. Through his death and resurrection, he made it possible for everyone, regardless of their past, to be reconciled to God.
- Praise God for Jesus, who made peace between us and God through his atoning work on the cross.

Peace-giver

Peace I leave with you; *my peace I give you.* I do not give to you as the world gives. Do not let your hearts be troubled and do not be afraid.

—John 14:27

- How great would it be to have the ability to give peace to any troubled person we meet? To be able to replace a person's fear, worry, or panic with peace would be wonderful. Alas, we do not have that ability.
- Jesus does. In the upper room, on the night he was betrayed, he promised his friends a peace that the world would neither give nor take away.
- The person, promise, and presence of Jesus enable us to live in peace. Praise God for Jesus and for his promise of peace for us.

Peacekeeper

You will *keep in perfect peace* him whose mind is steadfast, because he trusts in you.

—Isa 26:3

- The United Nations at times sends peacekeepers into hot spots around the world to maintain peace and order, often with limited success.
- God is a Peacekeeper. He is able to bring perfect peace to people's hearts when they do two things. First, trust in God. "God said it, I believe it, that settles it" is a good motto to live by. Second, to have a mind that is steadfastly anchored in those things that God has clearly promised in the Bible. The result of those two things is perfect peace.
- Praise God that perfect peace is available to us when we learn what God has said in the Bible and live as if it is true—which, of course, it is!

Piercer of Darkness

If I say, "Surely the darkness will hide me and the light become night around me," even the darkness will not be dark to you; the night will shine like the day, for *darkness is as light to you.*

—Pss 139:11–12

- Long before night-vision goggles were invented, God had the ability to see in total darkness. The darkest of nights is like noonday brightness to God. As amazing as night-vision goggles are, they cannot allow us to see like that.
- David's intent is to explain that no place is beyond God's all-seeing gaze. This is a comforting thought, for it means that it is impossible for us to be out of God's watchful gaze.
- Praise God for his watchful eye upon us.

Pity-causer

He caused them to be pitied by all who held them captive.

—Ps 106:46

- When Israel was taken captive into Babylon for seventy years in the time of Daniel, God worked in the hearts and minds of the captors so that they took pity on the Jews, giving them land and limited independence.
- God has the ability to move the hearts of people as he wishes. Surely, unbeknownst to the Babylonians, God was moving in their minds so that they thought it would be a good idea to treat their captives with kindness.
- God still works and moves in the hearts and minds of people—Christian and non-Christian alike—with equal ease.
- Praise God for his ability to work and move freely in people's hearts and minds.

Planner

> For I know the *plans* I have for you," declares the Lord, "*plans* to prosper you and not to harm you, *plans* to give you hope and a future.
>
> —JER 29:11

- God is a Planner.
- God's chastening love exiled the nation of Israel to Babylon for seventy years. But he was not done with them. He had plans for Israel—big plans. Plans to bless them and to give them a hopeful future.
- Just as God's covenant love was expressed in his plans to bless his people, Israel, he also has plans to bless his new covenant children—blessings attained through the atoning work of Jesus Christ.
- Praise God, who gives us this assurance: "being confident of this, that he who began a good work in you will carry it on to completion until the day of Christ Jesus" (Phil 1:6).
- Praise God that no Christian is too small or insignificant for God to have a plan for their life.

Plan-placer

He gave him *the plans of all that the Spirit had put in his mind* for the courts of the temple of the Lord and all the surrounding rooms, for the treasuries of the temple of God, and for the treasuries for the dedicated things.

—1 Chr 28:12

- King David had great plans in mind for a temple for God worthy of the Lord's greatness. However, God told him that his son Solomon would be the one to build it instead. So David handed off his plans to Solomon.
- Where did David get the ideas for this glorious temple in all its fine detail? From God, the Holy Spirit.
- God has the amazing ability to place in our heads his very thoughts and suggestions. When we pray for guidance or wisdom, we must pay careful attention to the resulting thoughts that come into our heads. They may be God's voice speaking to us. Of course, these ideas must be checked against the teachings of the Bible, God's only infallible guide for us.
- Praise God for his amazing ability to speak clearly into the human mind.

Portion-assigner

Lord, *you have assigned me my portion* and my cup; you have made my lot secure. The boundary lines have fallen for me in pleasant places; surely I have a delightful inheritance.

—Ps 16:5–6

- When we think of assignments, what comes to mind is usually a teacher telling students to turn in homework by a certain date or a military unit tasked with a special mission.
- The psalmist here talks about God assigning not a task, but a life situation. The psalmist looks at his life and sees that he has indeed been blessed. He considers the time and place in which he lives and realizes that it is only by God's providence that he is so blessed. If life could be compared to a piece of property, the psalmist states that his boundaries enclose a delightful plot.
- Praise God, who is our Portion-assigner, for your particular assignment. The portion most of us have been assigned has been good—far better than we deserve. Our devotion ebbs and flows, and yet God faithfully blesses us. How gracious is he!

Potter

Your hands shaped me and made me. Will you now turn and destroy me? Remember that *you molded me* like clay. Will you now turn me to dust again?

—JOB 10:8–9

Like clay in the hand of the *potter*, so are you in my hand, O house of Israel.

—JER 18:6B

- A potter takes a lump of formless clay and transforms it into a vessel of his or her choosing. Job argues with God that it makes no sense to make and mold him into the man he is only to destroy him through suffering and affliction.
- No potter makes a pot without a purpose in mind. God had a purpose in mind for Job's suffering, even though he chose to hide that purpose from Job.
- Praise God that he has made us for a purpose and for his glory. We are his workmanship, created in Christ Jesus to do the good works that God prepared in advance for us to do (Eph 2:10).
- Praise God for his ongoing shaping and transforming work in our lives.

Preserver

O Lord, you *preserve* both man and beast.

—Ps 36:6b

- The psalmist extols God for his love, faithfulness, righteousness, and justice (vv. 5–6), then declares confidently that God preserves both human and beast.
- When we think of "preserving" today, perhaps freezing or canning to protect against losing food to decay comes to mind. Or maybe we think of a life preserver, which enables a drowning person to be saved.
- God is our life preserver. We are kept safe in his powerful hands (John 10:28–29) and under his watchful eye. We need not fear because we are kept by our powerful, preserving God.

Procession-leader

But thanks be to God, who always *leads us in triumphal procession* in Christ and through us spreads everywhere the fragrance of the knowledge of him.

—2 Cor 2:14

- It is said that everyone loves a parade. That may be true, but this image tells of a parade like no other.
- Victorious Roman generals would lead their soldiers and captives through the city in a festive celebration while the crowds cheered and burned sweet spices in the streets.
- In just this way, the Christian, called to spiritual battle, is triumphantly led by God in Christ. The knowledge of Christ is the fragrance that spreads through the world.
- Praise God for the victory that is ours in Christ. We are on the winning side! All God's enemies have been defeated by Christ on the cross, and all that remains is to schedule the grand parade! In the meantime, we do not lose heart but instead continue to serve the Lord faithfully, helping spread the perfume of the gospel to a decaying world.

Promise-keeper

Not one of all the Lord's good promises to the house of Israel failed; *every one was fulfilled.*

—Josh 21:45

- Politicians make promises seemingly without any intention, or even ability, to keep them.
- People make promises lightly, fail to keep them, and then make excuses.
- Praise God that he keeps his promises.
- Some of God's promises: John 3:16; Matt 6:33; Phil 4:13; 1 Cor 10:13; 2 Cor 12:10; Matt 28:20; Heb 13:6–7.

Promise-maker

My comfort in my suffering is this: Your promise preserves my life . . . Your promises have been thoroughly tested, and your servant loves them.

—Pss 119:50, 140

- God is a promise-making and a promise-keeping God.
- The Bible is full of promises. If we reflect on the promises we find in the Bible and put them to the test, we will find ourselves in agreement with the psalmist—God keeps his word.
- Praise God for "his very great and precious promises" (2 Pet 1:4) and for Jesus, who is ultimately the fulfillment of all God's promises: "For no matter how many promises God has made, they are 'Yes' in Christ" (2 Cor 1:20a).

Promise-rememberer

For *he remembered his holy promise* given to his servant Abraham.

—Ps 105:42

- In the early chapters of the Bible, God made a covenant with Abraham—a covenant containing many promises not only to Abraham, but also to his descendants, and indeed to all the people of the world.
- Although we may forget some of our promises over time or fail to live up to them, God is faithful to each and every promise he has made.
- Praise God that he never forgets his promises. Each one will be honored.
- Of all his promises, none is greater than the fulfilled promise of a Savior, whose coming is unfolding in two stages. The first we read about in the pages of the Bible, and the second is promised in those same pages. Let's keep looking up!

Protector

Because he loves me," says the Lord, "I will rescue him; I will *protect* him, for he acknowledges my name.

—Ps 91:14

- The president of the United States has men and women whose primary job is to protect him. Sometimes, despite their best efforts, the president can be harmed or even killed.
- The psalmist extols the Lord's ability to protect those he loves. If the Lord wishes that no harm should befall his loved ones, then they shall indeed be safe, even if ten thousand others fall by their side. Sometimes God removes his protective hand from one he loves for purposes known only to him. This does not mean that his promise of protection has failed. We cannot be harmed apart from the Lord's allowing it.
- Praise God for his promise to protect us until it is time for us to go to heaven. Angels, in the meantime, are commissioned by God to guard and keep us day and night. Thus we can sleep in peace and face tomorrow without fear or dread.

Provider

But the Lord *provided* a great fish . . . the Lord *provided* a vine . . . God *provided* a worm . . . God *provided* a scorching east wind.

—Jonah 1:17a; 4:6a, 7a, 8a

- Jonah is a story of God's amazing patience with an obstinate man who did not care to serve God even though he was a follower of God.
- We see in the book of Jonah that God is master of fish, vines, worms, and winds. Each does God's bidding. Jonah needed these things so that God could instruct him in obedience and compassion for the lost people of Nineveh.
- God provides what we need, not necessarily what we want.
- Praise God, the master of all, including stubborn and disobedient hearts. Praise him too for his ways of correcting us when we say no to him.
- Praise God for providing us a needed Savior.

Quickener

But because of his great love for us, God, who is rich in mercy, *made us alive* with Christ even when we were dead in transgressions—it is by grace you have been saved.

—Eph 2:4–5

- The King James Version translates "made us alive" as "quickened us."
- Imagine what it must have been like in the cemetery the day when God summoned dead Lazarus from the tomb. Gasps and murmurs must have filled the air!
- Next time you drive by a cemetery try, to picture the day when God will quicken all who are in their graves and command them to boldly come forth. Won't that be a sight to behold!
- Praise God for his power to raise physically dead people to life. The greatest doctor in the world cannot make even one dead person live, yet God has the power to bring the dead to life. God is indeed in a league of his own!
- Praise God for the harder work of raising spiritually dead people to life. Even with our most persuasive arguments, we often find that we cannot make a person change their mind, let alone breathe life into their spiritually deadened soul. But God can and does. As you recall the day God did this work in your life, give thanks.

Quieter

On that day they will say to Jerusalem, "Do not fear, O Zion; do not let your hands hang limp. The Lord your God is with you, he is mighty to save. He will take great delight in you, *he will quiet you* with his love, he will rejoice over you with singing."

—Zeph 3:16–17

- If you picture a mother quieting her distressed baby, you will grasp the image of God that Zephaniah the prophet uses to describe God's tender love for his children. Israel is in the parental time-out chair for its sins, but God assures Israel of his continued love and care, which Israel will soon again experience once the time for chastening is past.
- Praise God for his tenderhearted manner of comforting and soothing his distressed and anxious children.

Raiser

He raises the poor from the dust and lifts the needy from the ash heap; he seats them with princes and has them inherit a throne of honor.

—1 Sam 2:8a

- When childless Hannah was granted a baby in response to her prayer, she in turn gave that boy, Samuel, back to God when he was older. In her prayer of thanks to God when she took Samuel to the temple, Hannah praised God for the help he gives to the poor and the needy, often turning around their fortunes.
- God is in the business of reversing things. Jesus said that when God sets all things right, the first will be last and the last will be first. And those who have little treasure in this life will have great treasure and honor in the life to come because of their simple trust in God, who alone is their resource in this world.
- Praise God for the great reversal that is coming, which Hannah foresaw.

Rampart

> He will cover you with his feathers, and under his wings you will find refuge; his faithfulness will be your shield and *rampart*.
>
> —Ps 91:4

- A rampart is a type of military defensive structure, usually an earthen embankment with a wall extending above it.
- The psalmist uses images of protection to describe the security of those who trust in God: "his faithfulness" will be all we need to keep us safe in times of danger.
- Praise God that we are safe because he loves us and shields us from harm behind the barricade of his protection.

Ransom

For even the Son of Man did not come to be served, but to serve, and to give his life a *ransom* for many.

—Mark 10:45

- In biblical days, the term "ransom" applied to the price paid to free a slave. In modern times, a ransom is a price paid by one person to free someone who has been captured or kidnapped.
- Jesus paid a ransom for us, who were "held prisoners by the law, locked up until faith should be revealed" (Gal 3:23b). The price paid was "not with perishable things such as silver and gold . . . but with the precious blood of Christ, a lamb without blemish or defect" (1 Pet 1:18–19).
- How we praise God for freeing us from our enslavement! How we brag and boast to all who will listen about the greatness of the One who went to such great lengths to free us from the prison of sin. Oh what love and grace has been extended to us.

Rebuker

Later Jesus appeared to the Eleven as they were eating; he *rebuked* them for their lack of faith and their stubborn refusal to believe those who had seen him after he had risen.

—MARK 16:14

- Love rebukes and corrects at times. This is one of those times for the disciples.
- Just as loving parents correct their children, God corrects us by confronting us when we do wrong. Sometimes the Holy Spirit uses the Bible to rebuke us. At other times God uses people, just as he used Nathan to confront King David in his sin.
- Praise God for his loving rebukes. Sin uncorrected harms us and sets a barrier between us and God. He loves us too much to allow that to happen.

Reconciler

All this is from God, who *reconciled us to himself through Christ* and gave us the ministry of reconciliation: that God was reconciling the world to himself in Christ, not counting men's sins against them. And he has committed to us the message of reconciliation.

—2 Cor 5:18–19

- A perpetual risk in relationships is estrangement. Things get said or done that drive a wedge between family members, friends, neighbors, colleagues, and even nations. Some choose to never speak to the offending party again.
- Reconciliation is needed so these broken relationships can be restored.
- When we sinned against God, we became estranged. It was really our place to initiate reconciliation by going to God to apologize and make amends. But in our stubbornness and pride, we would not. So God graciously took the initiative. He sent Jesus to repair our broken relationships and then, once we were reconciled, he appointed us as "reconciliation-agents" for the rest of the world. Praise God for his initiating love, for his valuing our relationship, and for paying the price to reconcile us.

Redeemer

Our great God and Savior, Jesus Christ, who gave himself for us *to redeem us from all wickedness and to purify for himself a people that are his very own, eager to do what is good.*

—TITUS 2:13B–14

- Sometimes when people need cash quickly, they take a valued possession to a pawnshop. They are paid some money, and the pawnshop holds their item for a period of time, during which the seller retains the right to come back to buy back—or redeem—the pawned item.
- Jesus paid the price to buy us back when we had sold ourselves into bondage by sin. His payment? "For you know that it was not with perishable things such as silver or gold that you were redeemed from the empty way of life handed down to you from your forefathers, but with the precious blood of Christ, a lamb without blemish or defect. He was chosen before the creation of the world, but was revealed in these last times for your sake. Through him you believe in God, who raised him from the dead and glorified him, and so your faith and hope are in God" (1 Pet 1:18–21).
- Praise God for his redeeming love.

Refiner

For you, O God, tested us; you *refined* us like silver.

—Ps 66:10

- Refining is a process by which extreme heat is applied to ore to separate the impurities from the precious metal contained within.
- God at times applies extreme heat (think of Job) to the lives of those he loves. We may think it cruel and unfair, but the intent is based in love. Some impurities in us will come out only when we are tempered in the furnace of affliction.
- Praise God for his refining love. Praise him too for his wisdom, which determines when and whether we need to experience the refining fire.

Refuge

The Lord is good, a *refuge* in times of trouble. He cares for those who trust in him.

—Nah 1:7

- The American government has established several wildlife refuges throughout the country where no hunting or fishing is allowed. As long as animals stay in the refuge boundaries, they are safe.
- God is a refuge for those who love and trust him. When we are in trouble, we can flee to him in prayer, pouring out our hearts, knowing that he cares for us. We can also cling to his written promises in the Bible, which remind us of the commitment God has made to us.

Repayer

Then Jesus said to his host, "When you give a luncheon or dinner, do not invite your friends, your brothers or relatives, or your rich neighbors; if you do, they may invite you back and so you will be repaid. But when you give a banquet, invite the poor, the crippled, the lame, the blind, and you will be blessed. Although they cannot repay you, *you will be repaid* at the resurrection of the righteous."

—Luke 14:12–14

- How is it possible to loan something to someone who literally has everything? Well, it can't be done—they have one of everything already. Yet that is the image God uses here. When we give of our material resources to those who are disadvantaged, God considers our giving as if we are lending to him. And he promises to repay us for the kindness we show.

- These verses echo Prov 19:17, which states, "He who is kind to the poor lends to the Lord, and he will reward him for what he has done."

- Praise God for his generous nature. He could just command us to help those in need without any expectation of recompense. Yet God promises that our helping the poor puts us in his debt in a sense. What an amazing God! How we should love and serve him!

Rescuer

Grace and peace to you from God our Father and the Lord Jesus Christ, who gave himself for our sins *to rescue us* from the present evil age, according to the will of our God and Father, to whom be glory for ever and ever. Amen.

—Gal 1:3–5

And to wait for his Son from heaven, whom he raised from the dead—Jesus, who *rescues us* from the coming wrath.

—1 Thess 1:10

- Some people are trained to rescue others who have been trapped in burning buildings, stranded on mountains, or lost in the wilderness. It is a fearful thing to be lost or trapped.
- Sometimes these rescuers lose their own lives while saving others.
- Jesus rescued us by giving up his life so that we might be safe—safe now, in this present evil age, and safe in the future, when the judgment of God falls upon sin and sinners.
- Praise God for Jesus, our Rescuer.

Rest-giver

He built up the fortified cities of Judah, since the land was at peace. No one was at war with him during those years, *for the Lord gave him rest.* "Let us build up these towns," he said to Judah, "and put walls around them, with towers, gates and bars. The land is still ours, because we have sought the Lord our God; we sought him and *he has given us rest* on every side." So they built and prospered . . . They sought God eagerly, and he was found by them. So *the Lord gave them rest* on every side.

—2 Chr 14:6–7; 15:15b

- Good King Asa was blessed by God, who gave him a break from war.
- God controls people and circumstances so that his purposes are accomplished. Here God works in the minds and lives of Israel's traditional enemies to keep them from wanting to attack King Asa. This ability is humanly impossible, but with God, all things are possible.
- Praise God for his ability to shield from the evil schemes of others all those he loves and who seek him eagerly (v. 15b).

Restorer

He restores my soul.

—Ps 23:3a

He must remain in heaven until the time comes for God to *restore everything*, as he promised long ago through his holy prophets.

—Acts 3:21

- Sheep have been known to unwisely lie down on an incline, roll over on their backs, and then get stuck like wooly turtles. The hapless sheep is helpless until the shepherd "restores" it to its feet. That may be the image behind shepherd David's familiar expression in the Twenty-third Psalm.
- God is our Restorer. When we find ourselves cast on our backs, God rescues and restores us.
- Praise God, who restores us now and who will in due time restore all things.

Revealer

He who forms the mountains, creates the wind, and *reveals his thoughts to man*, he who turns dawn to darkness, and treads the high places of the earth—the Lord God Almighty is his name.

—Amos 4:13

- Even for those whose lives are said to be an open book, the truth is that there are some private things in each of us that no one will ever know unless we tell them.
- To a far greater extent, there is much about God that we would never learn unless he told us. The varied and contradictory theological beliefs of the world's many religions illustrate what happens when humankind tries to guess God's thoughts.
- God has not left us to guess. He has revealed himself to the world through the glories of creation, through the Bible, and most clearly through his Son, the Lord Jesus.
- Praise God that we are not left to speculate as to the nature of God or what he expects of us. He wants us to know him and understand him: "but let him who boasts boast about this, that he understands and knows me" (Jer 9:24).

Rewarder

But as for you, be strong and do not give up, for your work *will be rewarded*.

—2 CHR 15:7

And without faith it is impossible to please God, because anyone who comes to him must believe that he exists and that he *rewards* those who earnestly seek him.

—HEB 11:6

- God sent an encouraging message to good King Asa, urging him to remain faithful. He also assured him that God would reward him for his faithfulness.
- A reward is not something earned but is a gift given in response to a good deed done.
- God is a rewarding God. If we were to take the time to study how often the Bible speaks of God rewarding those who love him, we might be surprised—it is an oft-repeated promise (see Matt 6:1–18, for example).
- Since God has the right to demand our service, anything that he chooses to promise us by way of reward is truly gracious. We are not entitled to any reward, yet God promises them over and over.
- Praise God for his generous heart in extending rewards to us when "we have only done our duty" (Luke 17:10).

Rich

But because of his great love for us, God, who is *rich in mercy*, made us alive with Christ even when we were dead in transgressions—it is by grace you have been saved.

—Eph 2:4–5

- Usually, the word "rich" is associated with money, lands, or possessions. We understand the concept—having abundance.
- God's riches extend beyond the physical. He is rich in grace, in kindness, and in mercy. He has an abundance of these riches, and his hand is open in generosity.
- God is merciful. He "does not treat us as our sins deserve or repay us according to our iniquities" (Ps 103:10).
- Praise God that he is not stingy when it comes to showing mercy. May his generosity to us prompt us "to act justly and to love mercy and to walk humbly with your God" (Mic 6:8).

Righteous

The Lord is righteous in all his ways and loving toward all he has made.

—Ps 145:17

- God alone is sinless and right in all that he thinks and does.
- We are so accustomed to living with flawed people that we are not surprised when they stumble or are discovered to have feet of clay.
- Praise God for his holy and righteous nature.
- Praise him too for his gift of righteousness to us through Jesus: " that I may gain Christ and be found in him, not having a righteousness of my own that comes from the law, but that which is through faith in Christ—the righteousness that comes from God and is by faith" (Phil 3:8–9) Although we still sin, in our standing before God we are declared to be righteous.

Rock

Be *my rock of refuge*, to which I can always go; give the command to save me, for you are *my rock* and my fortress.

—Ps 71:3

- Rocks represent that which is sturdy, strong, and immoveable and are often contrasted to sand or miry clay, both of which make it hard to stand securely.
- When we trust in God and his promises during difficult times, it is as if we are standing on an immoveable rock. We will not lose our footing or be washed away.
- Praise God that those who trust in him will be kept steady in times of trouble.
- Praise God for Jesus, "a chosen and precious cornerstone, and the one who trusts in him will never be put to shame. Now to you who believe, this stone is precious. But to those who do not believe, 'The stone the builders rejected has become the capstone'" (1 Pet 2:6b–7).

Ruler

The Lord has established his throne in heaven, and his kingdom *rules* over all.

—Ps 103:19

- "Who's in charge here?" is an expression we occasionally hear. When it comes to the world, God is in charge. He is the ruler and master of all. But what about Satan and the verse that says, "We know that we are children of God, and that the whole world is under the control of the evil one" (1 John 5:19)? As demonstrated in the book of Job, Satan has been granted freedom to work in this world, but always under the limitations God imposes on him. There is some mystery to all this, but the bottom line is that God is master and ruler of all, including of Satan and the forces of evil.
- Ponder the fact that God rules from his throne and that we are each part of that "all" over which he governs.

Sabbath-master

Then he said to them, "The Sabbath was made for man, not man for the Sabbath. So the Son of Man is *Lord even of the Sabbath.*"

—Mark 2:27–28

- When Jesus' disciples were criticized for violating the Sabbath day by picking heads of grain, rolling them in their hands, and eating the kernels, Jesus defended them by saying that since God made the Sabbath, God is the One who determines what violates it. Jesus then explained that the disciples were faultless in their behavior that day.
- God is master of every day of the week and every day of the year.
- Praise God for the Sabbath principle. This day of rest and worship is for our benefit and blessing. It was made to serve us and our needs, and we have liberty in deciding how best to use the day in a way that honors God.

Satisfier

> You open your hand and *satisfy* the desires of every living thing.
>
> —Ps 145:16

- The world is filled with living things, from large mammals to the smallest microscopic organisms. We know how to satisfy the desires of our pets. Farmers know how to satisfy the desires of their animals. But who can satisfy the desires of every living thing?
- How great is God that he not only imagined and created every living thing, but he also sustains and feeds them by simply opening his hand. How big must that hand be to satisfy the desires of all living things?
- We are some of those "living things" God made. His promise to us is that if we seek first his kingdom and his righteousness, then all our needs will be satisfied.
- Praise God, our Satisfier.

Savior

They said to the woman, "We no longer believe just because of what you said; now we have heard for ourselves, and we know that this man really is *the Savior of the world.*"

—JOHN 4:42

- When the townspeople checked in to the story of the woman at the well and heard Jesus speak, they concluded that indeed Jesus was no ordinary man. He was the Savior of the entire world.
- Saviors save people who are in need of saving. That would be every person in the world.
- Praise God for our salvation, and praise the One who keeps us safe from hell, judgment, and sin's destructive end.

Searcher

O Lord, you have *searched me* and you know me... *Search me*, O God, and know my heart; test me and know my anxious thoughts. See if there is any offensive way in me, and lead me in the way everlasting.

—Pss 139:1, 23–24

- In the computer age, we are familiar with programs that scan our hard drives and emails for anything that might be harmful and destructive.
- Similarly, the psalmist acknowledges that God is the ultimate scanner of the human heart and mind. David requests that God keep scanning his heart, well aware that he may be blind to the presence of sin-viruses lurking in the recesses of his life.
- Praise God, who, in his love for us, scans our lives to identify destructive "sin that so easily entangles" (Heb 12:1b).

Seed-supplier

Now *he who supplies seed* to the sower and bread for food will also *supply and increase your store of seed* and will enlarge the harvest of your righteousness.

—2 Cor 9:10

- Paul is using a farming analogy to teach about giving money to God's work. A farmer who sows many seeds will reap a greater harvest than the farmer who sows fewer seeds. The same is true in giving to God's work. Give more and you will reap more.

- God gives us our money in the first place ('he who supplies seed') and when we honor him by investing it in the Lord's work (planting it in the ground), God promises to give us more seed/money to plant in the future. It takes faith to give money to God's work but when we do, God promises to bless us.

- Praise God for his supply of seed/money and for the promise to bless us when we invest in God's kingdom work.

Seeker

I have strayed like a lost sheep. *Seek your servant,*
for I have not forgotten your commands.

—Psalm 119:176

For the Son of Man came *to seek* and to save what was lost.

—Luke 19:10

- When we lose something of little value, we don't look for it. We don't care. But when we lose something of great value, we search diligently until we find it.
- God loves and values us and thus seeks us when we are lost. In order to illustrate just how much God values every believer, Jesus told the story of a man with one hundred sheep who lost one. He left the ninety-nine and searched until he found it, returning with great joy to the fold.
- Praise God that he is still a seeking God today.

Sender

So then, it was not you who *sent me here*, but God.

—Gen 45:8a

- Joseph was sold into slavery by his own brothers, whose jealousy poisoned them against him. But Joseph came to understand that it was God, working in and through his brothers, who ultimately brought Joseph to Egypt. They were not absolved of their responsibility and guilt for their sin because it was their choice. Yet God worked such that his intention of getting Joseph to Egypt was also fulfilled. Although these things seem to contradict each other, they do not; they are compatible even if we struggle to see how.

- Praise God for his sovereign control of circumstances and the choices of people both good and bad, so that his will is never frustrated. Praise God for Jesus, who was sent from heaven on a mission of mercy to this world to redeem us and to restore our relationship with God.

- May our attitude of trust in God be expressed in the words of Isaiah: "Here am I. Send me!"

Servant

For even the Son of Man did not come to be served, but to serve, *and to give his life as a ransom for many.*

—MARK 10:45

- If asked whether they would rather serve or be served, most people would choose to be served. To many, serving others seems undignified. With the coming of Jesus, all that changed. Jesus honored all who work in the service professions through his life of service.
- If ever there was one who deserved to be served, it is Jesus. He was God come to earth in human form. His mission was to provide a service to those in need—to us. And what a service! We needed help in overcoming sin and the judgment that follows sin as surely as night follows day. So Jesus, the prophesied suffering servant of Isa 53, came to help us.
- Praise God for Jesus, our Leader, who models for us what it means to live a life of service to others.

Setter

But when God, who set me apart from birth and called me by his grace . . .

—Gal 1:15a

- Paul's testimony is that God had a plan and purpose for his life, ever since Paul was conceived in his mother's womb. God in some way set Paul aside when he was conceived, as if to say, "I have something special in mind for that one."
- Praise God that it is not only the Peters and the Pauls of this life who are set aside for God's special purposes. We all have been called by God to do the work "which God prepared in advance for us to do" (Eph 2:10b).

Shepherd

I am the good shepherd. The good shepherd lays down his life for the sheep.

—John 10:11

- Sheep have no means to protect themselves—no fangs, horns, claws, quills, or other weapons. They need someone to care for them. Sheep need a shepherd.
- We can be compared to sheep in that we need someone to care for us and help keep us safe from all harm, whether physical or spiritual.
- Not all shepherds care for the sheep under their protection. But Jesus is a good shepherd. In fact, he is such a benevolent shepherd that he is called "the Good Shepherd"—the template by which all other shepherds are measured.
- Praise God for Jesus, our Good Shepherd.

Shield

But *you are a shield* around me, O Lord; you bestow glory on me and lift up my head.

—Ps 3:3

He is a shield to those whose walk is blameless, for he guards the course of the just and protects the way of his faithful ones.

—Prov 2:7b–8

- Picture a soldier in biblical days on the battlefield with a sword in his right hand and a shield in his left. A soldier needed to learn how to use both effectively.
- God is likened to a shield that protects not just the soldier's left side, but also all "around me." No matter the direction of the attack, this Shield is positioned to protect us.
- Praise God that he is the Shield to those who are blameless. Being blameless does not mean that we have to be perfect, but rather that we are committed to love and serve God faithfully. When we trust in Christ, we are blameless in our standing with God because we have been clothed with the righteousness of Christ.
- Praise God that we do not need to live in fear of harm today from accident, from Satanic attack, from our own fleshly weakness, or from the world. God will protect us from all harm and allow into our life only what he intends to use for our refinement and his glory.

Shield

- Praise God for Jesus, who by his death on the cross shields us from the wrath of God, which remains on all those who reject the Son (John 3:36).

Sin-exposer

You have set our iniquities before you, *our secret sins in the light* of your presence.

—Ps 90:8

- It is human nature to try to hide our mistakes and our sins. But hidden sins produce guilt, fear, and shifting blame, harming our relationships. It is far better for sin to be confessed so forgiveness can be sought and granted.
- Moses declared that the all-knowing God brings our hidden, secret sins into the open, where we must deal with God's righteous wrath: "All our days pass away under your wrath; we finish our years with a moan" (v. 9).
- Our sins expose us to God's anger and judgment. We have a right to be "consumed by your anger and terrified by your indignation" (v. 7). How can we expect anything else from a holy God?
- Praise God for Jesus, who bore the wrath of God against sin—our sin—on the cross. Our exposed sins have been forever taken from us by the great act of Jesus' loving death on the cross: "He himself bore our sins in his body on the tree, so that we might die to sins and live for righteousness; by his wounds you have been healed" (1 Pet 2:24).

Singer

On that day they will say to Jerusalem, "Do not fear, O Zion; do not let your hands hang limp. The Lord your God is with you, he is mighty to save. He will take great delight in you, he will quiet you with his love, *he will rejoice over you with singing.*"

—Zeph 3:17–18

- We often sing when we are happy and our hearts are filled with joy.
- God is so delighted with his people that he sings over them, much like a loving mother sings a lullaby over her sleeping baby.
- Reflect and give praise to our God, whose love for us is so deep that it expresses itself in God's joyful singing.

Sin-remover

As far as the east is from the west, so far has he *removed our transgressions* from us.

—Ps 103:12

Look, the Lamb of God, who *takes away the sin of the world!*

—John 1:29b

- On the Day of Atonement, the high priest laid his hands on the head of a live goat and confessed all the sins of the nation over it before he drove the goat away into the wilderness, where it would symbolically carry away the sin of the people.
- We are powerless to remove even one sin from our lives. Hoping God will forget our sins or that our good deeds will somehow cancel out our bad deeds is foolish. There is only one way to removes sins, and that is through Jesus, the Lamb of God.
- Praise God that our sins have been borne away by Jesus, even those we, regrettably, will commit in the future. Thank you, Jesus!

Sin-restrainer

Direct my footsteps according to your word; *let no sin rule over me.*

—Ps 119:133

- One of the realities of life is that sin has an addictive and binding power. It is not easily overcome, but it can be conquered by God's grace and power.
- God not only has the power to break sin's grip on us, he has the power prevent sin from enslaving us in the first place. The psalmist recognizes his need for God's assistance in keeping free from the sin that so easily entangles.
- Praise God for both his ability to break sin's power and his ability to shield us from its dominating control.

Sin-treader

Who is a God like you, who pardons sin and forgives the transgression of the remnant of his inheritance? You do not stay angry forever but delight to show mercy. You will again have compassion on us; you *will tread our sins underfoot and hurl all our iniquities into the depths of the sea.*

—Mic 7:18–19

- Many of us stomp on spiders, ants, and other insects when we find them in our homes.
- Treading is a sign of domination. God grinds our sins into the ground, destroying them.
- Praise God for his ability and desire to destroy our sins, compassionately choosing not to hold them against us, even at great cost to himself. Jesus bore our sins himself on the cross, effectively treading them underfoot. What an encouraging image!

Sleep-granter

In vain you rise early and stay up late, toiling for food to eat—for *he grants sleep* to those he loves.

—Ps 127:2

- Human plans are all in vain unless the Lord blesses our efforts. Burning the candle at both ends is not the key to success; our success depends on God blessing our labors: "Now listen, you who say, 'Today or tomorrow we will go to this or that city, spend a year there, carry on business and make money.' Why, you do not even know what will happen tomorrow. Instead, you ought to say, 'If it is the Lord's will, we will live and do this or that'" (Jas 4:13–15).

- We should plan well, work hard, and then leave the results to God. To lay awake at night worrying shows a lack of faith in God. When we let God do the worrying, we are able to sleep.

- Praise God for his sovereign control and supervision of our plans. Hear Jesus say, in a paraphrase to Matt 6:34, "Go to sleep and don't worry about tomorrow. We will deal with tomorrow when it gets here."

Song

The Lord is my strength and *my song*; he has become my salvation.

—Ps 118:14

- New songs are composed to celebrate special occasions and express joy. Sometimes the old songs are just not good enough to celebrate the new event properly, so we "Sing to the Lord a new song" (Ps 98:1).
- The psalmist sings a song of joy, celebrating the goodness of God because "the Lord helped me" (v. 13). God's help calls for a new song extolling God's provision.
- In thanks for all the Lord has done for us, we should be regularly composing new songs of praise to God.
- Praise God for all he has done and for putting a new song in our mouths.

Sparrow-rememberer

Are not five sparrows sold for two pennies? Yet *not one of them is forgotten by God*. Indeed, the very hairs of your head are all numbered. Don't be afraid; you are worth more than many sparrows.

—Luke 12:6–7

- In biblical times, sparrows were commonly sold cheaply for food. Despite the fact that sparrows were inexpensive and seemingly insignificant, God sees and knows about each.
- God's knowledge of all things is expansive and complete, even down to the minutest detail of life. He is watchfully aware of what is happening to all his creation.
- We can live free from fear because God values us and watches over us—and our value is much greater than that of sparrows.
- Praise God for his sovereign watchfulness over us, enabling us to live without fear.

Spirit-sender

But I tell you the truth: It is for your good that I am going away. Unless I go away, the Counselor will not come to you; but if I go, *I will send him* to you.

—John 16:7

- In times of disaster and great need, the call goes out for aid, and soon skilled people respond.
- After his atoning work on earth was completed, Jesus ascended to heaven, but knowing that his disciples would need his help, he and the Father sent God the Holy Spirit to be with us as our Helper.
- Praise God that we have not been left as orphans but are fortunate enough to have the presence of God with us in the Holy Spirit. How amazing that God actually lives inside us!

Stooper

You give me your shield of victory, and your right hand sustains me; *you stoop down* to make me great.

—Ps 18:35

Who is like the Lord our God, the One who sits enthroned on high, *who stoops down* to look on the heavens and the earth?

—Ps 113:5–6

- It is heartwarming to see an adult stoop down to talk with a child.
- If we think of God spatially, we realize that to him, even the earth and skies are small, much less people. We are ant-like in size, and yet God stoops to attend to us and to honor us.
- Praise God for his greatness in condescending to stoop down to us. Moreover, marvel at his greatness in becoming one of us to rescue us from sin, death, and hell.

Strengthener

I pray that out of his glorious riches *he may strengthen you* with power through his Spirit in your inner being.

—Eph 3:16

God is our refuge and *strength*, an ever-present help in trouble.

—Ps 46:1

- How nice would it be to have an endless supply of power to share with those who are weak or worn down by old age, sickness, grief, and struggles with sin?
- God has the ability to give strength to the weak by his indwelling Holy Spirit. God's very power is channeled into us in some mysterious but real way.
- Praise God for his willingness to give strength to those he loves.
- See also Ps 86:16; 119:28; Hab 3:19.

Striker

But David said to Abishai, "Don't destroy him! Who can lay a hand on the Lord's anointed and be guiltless? As surely as the Lord lives," he said, "the Lord himself *will strike him*; either his time will come and he will die, or he will go into battle and perish."

—1 Sam 26:9–10

- David, wrongly pursued by Saul, has an opportunity to kill his adversary. Abishai knows David has been anointed by God as the rightful king, yet David restrains his cousin from killing the king, who is rebelling against God. David knows that God will remove Saul in his own time and that God has not authorized him to do it.
- Every person living will die as a result of God's judgment on humanity for its sin. God literally holds the fate of each of us in his hand and will summon us from this world at the time of his choosing.
- Praise God that our lives are safely tucked into the protective and loving hand of God: "My times are in your hands; deliver me from my enemies and from those who pursue me" (Ps 31:15).

Strong

One thing God has spoken, two things have I heard: that *you, O God, are strong*, and that you, O Lord, are loving. Surely you will reward each person according to what he has done.

—Ps 62:11–12

- Strength comes in various forms—physical, emotional, and volitional (i.e., willpower) all come to mind.
- However strength is measured, God is strong—stronger than anyone or anything else. By his might, the universe was created. By his strength, Jesus was raised from the dead. By his power, Satan and all God's enemies shall be defeated.
- The children's chorus is true: "My God is so big, so strong and so mighty, there is nothing my God cannot do."
- Praise God for his mighty power, which is available to all who put their trust in him: "grant your strength to your servant" (Ps 86:16).

Stronghold

The Lord is my light and my salvation—whom shall I fear? The Lord is *the stronghold of my life*—of whom shall I be afraid?

—Ps 27:1

- A stronghold conveys the image of a well-fortified position that affords safety from attack.
- We all face many kinds of danger in life, but none greater than that of our spiritual foe, Satan and his evil minions: "Be self-controlled and alert. Your enemy, the devil, prowls around like a roaring lion looking for someone to devour" (1 Pet 5:8).
- Praise God for affording us safety in the Lord Jesus, our Stronghold.

Sustainer

Surely God is my help; the Lord is the one *who sustains me.*

—Ps 54:4

- When David was running for his life from murderous King Saul, he was betrayed by people he trusted. He wrote this song in response to that betrayal, crying out to God and expressing confidence in God, his Sustainer.
- All living things need sustenance.
- Whether facing murderous threats, malicious gossip, sickness, financial woes, or just our daily needs, God is our Sustainer. This truth gives us the peace and confidence to face each day.
- Praise God, who is committed to meeting our needs today, tomorrow, and forever. Praise him too that he will provide us all that we need to carry out our work on earth.

Sweeper and Turner

You turn men back to dust, saying, "Return to dust, O sons of men"... *You sweep men away* in the sleep of death; they are like the new grass of the morning, though in the morning it springs up new, by evening it is dry and withered."

—Ps 90:3, 5

- Moses' image here is one of sweeping grass clippings from the walkway.
- God told Adam, "Dust you are, and to dust you will return" (Gen 3:19b).
- We are not at the mercy of chance, fate, accidents, or the schemes of wicked people. God is the One who sweeps us from this world into eternity. Jesus admonished us, "Do not be afraid of those who kill the body but cannot kill the soul. Rather, be afraid of the One who can destroy both soul and body in hell" (Matt 10:28).
- Praise God that our lives and times are in the hands of our loving, wise Father in heaven.

Sword

Blessed are you, O Israel! Who is like you, a people saved by the Lord? He is your shield and helper and your glorious sword. Your enemies will cower before you, and you will trample down their high places.

—Deut 33:29

- These words of blessing, which Moses gave to the nation of Israel before they entered the promised land, may sound strange to us now. The promise is that God will drive out the wicked inhabitants of the land, using Israel's army as his sword of judgment.
- The world today has powerful and wicked nations that oppress, kill, starve, imprison, and exploit the weak and vulnerable among their people. God will one day bring judgment upon these nations in the only terms they understand—might and power.
- The triumphantly returning Lord Jesus is portrayed in the book of Revelation as a mighty warrior: "Out of his mouth comes a sharp sword with which to strike down the nations. He will rule them with an iron scepter. He treads the winepress of the fury of the wrath of God Almighty" (Rev 19:15).
- Praise God that he will use whatever means necessary to protect and provide for those he loves.

Task-assigner

What, after all, is Apollos? And what is Paul? Only servants, through whom you came to believe—as *the Lord has assigned to each his task*. I planted the seed, Apollos watered it, but God made it grow.

—1 Cor 3:5–6

- Paul is correcting the Corinthian Christians, who were dividing the church over conflicting loyalty to various leaders. Paul argues that we are all on the same team, and the One who should get the credit is God.
- The director of a play tells the actors their roles, positions, and lines. Some have a more visible role than others.
- On a military mission, each soldier is assigned a specific task, and the success of the mission depends on every person in the unit doing his or her part.
- God assigns us our work, giving each of us the gift of working as part of the body of Christ while we each serve the kingdom mission.
- Praise God, who assigns us our tasks in his service according to how we can best advance his kingdom work.

Teacher

Teach me knowledge and good judgment, for I believe in your commands.

—Ps 119:66

- Good teachers impart facts and information, but they also show their students how to live out what they teach.
- God is a Teacher, and we are his students. However, his teaching rarely happens in a classroom. The world is his classroom. He follows us wherever we go and uses our life experiences to teach us how to grow in grace, in faith, and in the likeness of Jesus.
- What a privilege it is to sit under the teaching of Jesus, the greatest Teacher of all time!
- Praise God that he is willing to have us as his students (the Greek work for "disciple" means "learner").
- Praise him too for the Bible, in which his commands are recorded for our instruction.

Tester

For you, O God, tested us; you refined us like silver. You brought us into prison and laid burdens on our backs. You let men ride over our heads; we went through fire and water, but you brought us to a place of abundance.

—Ps 66:10–12

- We associate tests with school and teachers—and likely stress as well!
- Teachers give tests for the benefit of the students, so as to reveal their level of mastery of their subject—or lack thereof. Then both teacher and student can team up to fortify that area of weakness.
- Similarly, God's love for us compels him to test us so that any sin or weakness will be exposed in us. Then he will work with us to address these shortcomings.
- Whereas a teacher might set one test for an entire class, God's tests are individualized. My test may look nothing like the person's next to me because we each need different things.
- Praise God for his tests, even though they can be stressful and challenging at times.
- Praise God for Jesus, who was tested more than any other. Yet no sin was found in him. Because he suffered when he was tested (the same word as "tempted" in biblical Greek), "he is able to help those who are being tempted" (Heb 2:18).
- See also Deut 8:2, 14, 16.

Thinker

Yet I am poor and needy; may the *Lord think of me*. You are my help and my deliverer; O my God, do not delay.

—Ps 40:17

- Thoughts of those we love often cross our minds.
- Each of us has met countless people in our lifetimes. Many are forgotten. And of those people we can recall, we often go for long periods without thinking about them at all.
- With God, we are never forgotten. He never has to stop and ask, "Now who are you again?" or "Where do I know you from?" He remembers us and thinks of us always.
- Praise God that even though he knows billions of people, God is never too busy to think of us today.

Thirst-quencher

Jesus answered, "Everyone who drinks this water will be thirsty again, but whoever drinks the water I give him *will never thirst*. Indeed, the water I give him will become in him a spring of water welling up to eternal life."

—John 4:13–14

- Nothing is more refreshing than a drink of cold water when we are parched from work, play, or exercise. The woman Jesus encountered at the well in Samaria mistakenly thought Jesus was offering her this kind of water.
- Not all our thirsts are for liquid. Our hearts and souls long for the fulfillment and satisfaction that is drawn from a different kind of well.
- Praise God for his ability to satisfy the deepest longings and desires of the human heart. He is indeed the living water.
- Praise God too that Jesus, our living water, was poured out for us on the cross.

Thorn-giver

To keep me from becoming conceited because of these surpassingly great revelations, there was given to me *a thorn in my flesh*, a messenger of Satan, to torment me. Three times I pleaded with the Lord to take it away from me. But he said to me, "My grace is sufficient for you, for my power is made perfect in weakness." Therefore I will boast all the more gladly about my weaknesses, so that Christ's power may rest on me.

—2 Cor 12:7–9

- God gave the Apostle Paul some amazing visions, granting him a peek into the heavenly world. To prevent Paul from becoming conceited over this privilege, God afflicted Paul with what was likely a medical condition. Once Paul realized that this 'thorn' was from God, using Satan as his delivery system, Paul accepted it and even rejoiced in it because it made it all the more obvious to others that God's power was what enabled Paul to accomplish all that he did.
- God gives thorns to his children as he sees fit. He is so determined that we not fall into sinful habits or attitudes that he will use whatever means are helpful in keeping us on track spiritually.
- Praise God for his wisdom in knowing what we need to grow in our faith and to keep us close to him.
- Praise God that our weakness can be a platform for God to work in and through us.

Thought-evaluator

The Lord detests the *thoughts* of the wicked, but those of the pure are pleasing to him.

—Prov 15:26

- We often hear expressions like "a penny for your thoughts" and "it's the thought that counts."
- A person's heart is his or her private domain—it can be screened off from even the most inquisitive and prying eyes. Yet God peers into every heart, evaluating the thoughts he finds there.
- Pure hearts produce pure thoughts. Sinful hearts yield thoughts that are displeasing to God.
- How pleasant it is to know that we can bring pleasure to God by having pure hearts that give rise to thoughts that make him smile.
- Praise God that he cares about our thoughts and takes pleasure in them.

Thunderer

The voice of the Lord is over the waters; *the God of glory thunders,* the Lord *thunders* over the mighty waters. The voice of the Lord is powerful; the voice of the Lord is majestic. The voice of the Lord breaks the cedars; the Lord breaks in pieces the cedars of Lebanon ... The voice of the Lord strikes with flashes of lightning. The voice of the Lord shakes the desert ... The voice of the Lord twists the oaks and strips the forests bare. And in his temple all cry, "Glory!"

—Pss 29:3–5, 7, 8a, 9

- The power of nature unleashed is impressive, perhaps never more so than with God's light and sound shows: thunderstorms.
- God's voice is as powerful as any force of nature, even a tornado that strips limbs from trees, leaving only twisted trunks and stumps.
- God's power is rarely seen, although nature's rage is a reminder of the One whose merest word can tear up the earth.
- Reflect on the most impressively powerful display of nature you can recall, and see in it the might of God, who loves and cares for you. This God, like Jesus on the Sea of Galilee, commands nature to do his bidding.

Tower

From the ends of the earth I call to you, I call as my heart grows faint; lead me to the rock that is higher than I. For you have been my refuge, *a strong tower* against the foe.

—Ps 61:2–3

- The word "castle" evokes images of moats, drawbridges, and stone towers. In an era of bows, spears, and swords, a strong tower was a place of security where people could retreat to safety in times of attack.
- We need a strong tower to flee to in more than just times of war. In our daily lives, we get worn down by the pressures of life such that, like the psalmist, we long for a place of retreat.
- God is our Tower of safety and solace. He will meet us there and grant us refreshment.

Trainer

Praise be to the Lord, my Rock, *who trains my hands for war*, my fingers for battle.

—Ps 144:1

- King David was God's man, ruling over Israel as his representative.
- Attacks on Israel's kings were considered an attack on God, Israel's King. God's response came through the army led by his regent king, David, who acknowledged God's role in equipping him to carry out God's military response.
- God equips us to do what he calls us to do. Just as he trained David to be the general of his army, he trains us to do whatever work he has in mind for us to do in his service. He knows our unique abilities, aptitudes, and skills, and he hones them so that we can be effective in our ministries.
- Praise God that we have a personal Trainer who is constantly fitting us for service in the kingdom.

Tree

O Ephraim, what more have I to do with idols? I will answer him and care for him. *I am like a green pine tree*; your fruitfulness comes from me.

—Hos 14:8

- Because of Israel's persistent disobedience to God's laws and covenant, God punished them by summoning a pagan nation to overthrow them. God promised that if Israel repented, he would bless them once again and make them fruitful. God uses the imagery of trees to illustrate something of himself.
- Comparisons of mighty kings to trees are found in a few places in the Bible. For example, in the time of Daniel, God likened the pagan Babylonian king Nebuchadnezzar to a giant tree: "Its leaves were beautiful, its fruit abundant, and on it was food for all. Under it the beasts of the field found shelter, and the birds of the air lived in its branches; from it every creature was fed" (Dan 4:12).
- God is similarly likened to a tree that is green, full of life, and a source of food and safety for Israel.
- Reflect on the imagery of God as an enormous tree in which you and all the world can find safe haven.

Troubler of Nations

In those days it was not safe to travel about, for all the inhabitants of the lands were in great turmoil. One nation was being crushed by another and one city by another, because *God was troubling them* with every kind of distress.

—2 Chr 15:5–6

- God sent the prophet Azariah to encourage King Asa, promising to bless him if he continued to institute religious and moral reforms in the land. He said that God stirred up trouble in the world so as to turn people's hearts toward him.
- God has the ability to cause political, military, and social upheaval in any town, state, nation, or even worldwide if it serves his purposes.
- Praise God for his ability to stir upheaval and to remove it. How much of the world's troubles today are the direct result of God's troubling work? Is he trying to get our attention by withdrawing his restraining hand against sin and allowing people to do what their sinful hearts naturally do?
- Praise God for his patience and restraint with the sinfulness of humankind and for his willingness to give people an incentive to repent so they too can experience his blessing.

Truth

Jesus answered, "I am the way and *the truth* and the life. No one comes to the Father except through me."

—John 14:6

- Truth in advertising and politics is elusive. We become cynical, sensing that everyone has an agenda and selectively uses facts to manipulate us.
- It is so refreshing when we find a politician who commends an opponent for a good idea or an advertiser who acknowledges that their competitor has a worthy product.
- Jesus always spoke the truth, so much so that his name was synonymous with the truth. He never manipulated. He was never selective with the facts or misleading. He had no hidden agenda. He just spoke the truth and let people take it or leave it.
- Rejoice in the One whose every word is truth and who can be trusted absolutely.

Unchanging

Every good and perfect gift is from above, coming down from the Father of the heavenly lights, who does not change like shifting shadows.

—Jas 1:17

- It is said that the only constant in this world is change. Some changes are celebrated, while others are mourned.
- Regrettably, some people change in how they feel or act towards others. Husbands change and stop loving their wives. Friends change so that the closeness between them is lost.
- It is reassuring to know that God never changes. We can depend on him always being the same, regardless of the passing of time.
- Praise God that in a world where everything changes, he does not. When we are old and withered, we will still find his loving ways to be exactly as they were when we first knew him.
- Praise God that our God is "the same yesterday and today and forever" (Heb 13:8).

Understanding-giver

Your statutes are forever right; *give me understanding* that I may live.

—Ps 119:144

- We are limited in our understanding; there is much we do not know.
- Wouldn't it be nice to be able to give our children an understanding of how the world works, whom to trust, and how to make the right choices? The difficulty is that we don't always have the answers ourselves!
- God is able to give us understanding and wisdom. When we are perplexed or unsure of what to do, we can go to him and gain understanding. Now, this understanding is not given merely for the asking. God recognizes that sometimes it is better for us to wrestle through certain issues or to try to figure out things on our own using the principles and teachings he gave us in the Bible.
- The Bible is God's primary way of giving us understanding. As we read and reflect on it, we will find the Holy Spirit bringing thoughts to our minds that help us make good decisions.
- Praise God for his gift of understanding.

Unfailing Lover

Within your temple, O God, we meditate on your unfailing love.

—Ps 48:9

- We live in a world where many things fail—our health, our cars, politicians' promises, sump pumps, hard drives, or marriage vows. We come to expect it.
- Yet God's love never fails. Change will never happen on his end, for he is changeless. Change will not happen on our end either, in that when we inevitably stumble and sin, he will not abandon us.
- Praise God for his unfailing love. We are reassured with the knowledge that when we commit our lives into his care and keeping, his love for us is unchanging and unfailing.

Unity-giver

May the God who gives endurance and encouragement *give you a spirit of unity among yourselves as you follow Christ Jesus, so that with one heart and mouth you may glorify the God and Father of our Lord Jesus Christ.*

—Rom 15:5–6

- Can you imagine the fame, popularity, and value of a person who could unite warring individuals, families, churches, teams, and nations despite their differences? Such a person could run for president of the world! His or her ability would indeed revolutionize the world! One thing is clear: this person would be kept quite busy.
- God has that ability, and he uses it in the lives of those whose ears are tuned to his voice.
- Paul wrote to a congregation in which significant differences had arisen. His prayer of blessing for that church was that they might receive from God the endurance, encouragement, and spirit of unity they needed so they could "with one heart and mouth . . . glorify the God and Father of the Lord Jesus Christ" (v. 6).
- Praise God for his wondrous ability to knit into one fabric the divergent threads of opinion and belief among his people.

Upholder

The Lord upholds all those who fall and lifts up all who are bowed down.

—Ps 145:14

- We can think of people who benefit from a strong arm to lean on—the elderly, those recovering from injury, and those carrying great burdens. We can help with these kinds of needs.
- In a spiritual sense, we find ourselves in need of someone to hold us up whenever we are discouraged, wounded, fearful, or in grief. We find it much more challenging to step in to help with these kinds of needs.
- God is able to give an inner power to those who are hard-pressed and weighed down.
- "No temptation has seized you except what is common to man. And God is faithful; he will not let you be tempted beyond what you can bear. But when you are tempted, he will also provide a way out *so that you can stand up under it*" (1 Cor 10:13).
- Praise God for his strong arms that hold us up.

Victory-giver

He holds victory in store for the upright, he is a shield to those whose walk is blameless, for he guards the course of the just and protects the path of his faithful ones.

—Prov 2:7–8

- Sports fans root for their team to win crucial games. Parents cheer on their children, hoping they will be able to savor the sweet taste of victory on the playing field.
- Wouldn't it be nice to be able to keep victory in your pocket so you could pull it out and dispense it at just that right time? But alas (or maybe thankfully), we do not have that ability.
- But God can and does give victory to those who are blameless—his children. Sometimes, that victory takes the shape of success in overcoming opposition and challenges in life, and at other times, it is expressed in death, or the taking of the godly to heaven.
- Praise God, in whose hand is victory, dispensed wisely and lovingly to each of his dear children.

Vine

I am the true vine, and my Father is the gardener . . . *I am the vine*; you are the branches. If a man remains in me and I in him, he will bear much fruit; apart from me you can do nothing.

—John 15:1, 5

- The grape vine sprouts branches along its length. From those branches grow the grapes. The life-giving sap flows from the vine through these branches to the grapes.
- Jesus describes himself as the "true vine," implying there are other vines out there that are not "true." The key to a fruitful life—a life we live in a way that is pleasing to God—is being attached to God.
- A life spent apart from God and his life-giving presence is a life that, in the end, will have fallen short of its potential.
- Praise God, who is pleased to have people like us as his branches. Praise him too for the fruit that is slowly and often imperceptibly growing in us.

Waiter

It will be good for those servants whose master finds them watching when he comes. I tell you the truth, he will dress himself to serve, will have them recline at the table and will come and *wait on them.*

—Luke 12:37

- Has a restaurant owner ever sat his or her staff down for a meal and waited on them as a way to express his thanks? Maybe it has happened somewhere.
- Has a CEO ever come to the home of his or her janitorial help to clean their bathrooms? Less likely.
- Has a homeowner ever gone to the homes of his or her gardeners and cut their grass?
- Yet here, the Master of the universe is said to dress himself in servant garb and wait upon his servants. It is unbelievable! How can this be?
- Remembering the incarnation, when God assumed human flesh and dwelt among us (Mark 10:45), did he not say that he came to serve rather than be served?
- How great is our God! This teaching reveals his gracious and loving heart. We are not only servants, we are unworthy servants (Luke 17:10), and yet God honors us in this way.
- Reflect on both our own unworthiness and God's grace, and praise him!

Watcher

He will not let your foot slip—he who *watches over you* will not slumber... *The Lord watches over you*... The Lord will keep you from all harm—*he will watch over your life; the Lord will watch over* your coming and going both now and forevermore.

—Ps 121:3, 5a, 7–8

The Lord watches over all who love him, but all the wicked he will destroy.

—Ps 145:20

- As the psalmist makes his way up to Jerusalem to worship God at the temple, he sings this song of confidence, an ode to the watchful care of God.
- There is a kind of watching that is passive, by which we sit and observe (e.g., TV, movies, sports), but there is also an active kind of watching (e.g., a toddler in the wading pool).
- God's watching is the active kind. He attentively watches over all those he loves, guarding and protecting them as he directs their lives.
- Praise God for his watchful care over us and over those we love.

Whistler

He lifts up a banner for the distant nations, *he whistles* for those at the ends of the earth. Here they come, swiftly and speedily!

—Isa 5:26

In that day *the Lord will whistle* for flies from the distant streams of Egypt and for bees from the land of Assyria.

—Isa 7:18

- Just as people whistle for trained dogs to come on command, the Lord whistles for his trained dogs (the Assyrian army) to come do his bidding, namely to chasten God's chosen people, Israel.
- Praise God for his sovereign power. All powers, both good and evil, are under his command. The Assyrian king and military exercise their freedom to choose to attack Israel while God simultaneously exercises his right to have them do his bidding at the precise time he wishes. Although seemingly incompatible, these two realities exist side by side in Scripture. Only God is big enough to make the seemingly incompatible, compatible.
- Praise God that all things bend to his will and that he can summon any person to do his bidding at will.

Wisdom-giver

Because the patriarchs were jealous of Joseph, they sold him as a slave into Egypt. But God was with him and rescued him from all his troubles. *He gave Joseph wisdom* and enabled him to gain the goodwill of Pharaoh of Egypt; so he made him ruler over Egypt and all his palace.

—Acts 7:9–10

- We all struggle to know what to do at times. We want to make the best decision, so we do all in our power to find the right and wise choice.
- God has an endless supply of wisdom, and he gives it to those who please him and who ask in faith: "If any of you lacks wisdom, he should ask God, who gives generously to all without finding fault, and it will be given to him. But when he asks, he must believe and not doubt" (Jas 1:5–6a).
- Joseph faced a series of predicaments that would have stumped the best of us—he was tossed in a pit, sold into slavery, falsely accused by his boss's wife, falsely imprisoned, and forgotten by the cupbearer. Through it all, God directed his thinking so that Joseph's decisions were wise, and God's purposes unfolded at just the right time.
- Praise our wisdom-giving God, who waits for us to ask.

Wise

Oh, the depth of the riches of the *wisdom* and knowledge of God! How unsearchable his judgments, and his paths beyond tracing out!

—Rom 11:33

- This statement is part of a grand declaration of praise to God given by the Apostle Paul after he detailed God's plan to reconcile Jews and Gentiles through Christ. God's wisdom is on display through the cross.
- The wisest man who lived prior to Jesus was Solomon, whom God gifted with wisdom beyond all others. But the wisdom of God exceeds that of Solomon and we can trust in it.
- Reflect on the wisdom of God and applaud him for it: "For my thoughts are not your thoughts, neither are your ways my ways," declares the Lord. "As the heavens are higher than the earth, so are my ways higher than your ways and my thoughts than your thoughts" (Isa 55:8–9).

Womb-opener

Then God remembered Rachel; he listened to her and *opened her womb*.

—GEN 30:22

- This verse comes from a tale of two sisters competing for the love of the same man. When God saw that Leah was unloved, he opened her womb and closed the womb of her more attractive sister, Rachel (Gen 30:2).
- For couples unable to conceive, the longing for a child is intense, and the inability to have a baby is heartbreaking. Yet even here, we are reminded that God is sovereign and opens and closes wombs as he pleases. God's control extends everywhere, including into the most secret innermost places. He is able, by a word, to prevent conception or to enable it.
- Our fallen world produces couples unable to conceive. At times, God overrides this consequence of the fall (Gen 3), while at other times he does not, for reasons known only to him.
- Praise God for his oversight of the miracle of conception, even as we pray for God to open the wombs of women we know who long to have a baby.

Worker

Jesus said to them, "*My Father is always at his work* to this very day, and I, too, am working."

—JOHN 5:17

- Jesus was criticized for much of what he said and did. On this occasion, he healed a man who had been an invalid for thirty-eight years on the Sabbath.
- In response to such criticism, Jesus said that since God works seven days a week, so can he.
- What kind of work does God do that keeps him busy seven days a week? Sustaining and directing the affairs of the universe would certainly be part of that. Maintaining oversight over every circumstance for each person in the world must take time as well: "And we know that in all things God works" (Rom 8:28a).
- Reflect on the fact that our God is actively working in the world, then find out what he is doing and join him.
- Praise God for his work, even if it is sometimes hidden from view, in our lives.

Wounder

See now that I myself am he! There is no god besides me. I put to death and I bring to life, *I have wounded* and I will heal, and no one can deliver out of my hand.

—Deut 32:39

For they persecute *those you wound* and talk about the pain of those *you hurt*.

—Ps 69:26

- It is a strange thing to consider that God sometimes wounds people. How are we to understand this?
- Sometimes love requires us to hurt the people we love. As Prov 27:6 states, "Wounds from a friend can be trusted, but an enemy multiplies kisses." At times, the only thing that gets through to us is a figurative slap in the face—a wound. Without it, we would continue to do things that are harmful, sinful, or stupid to ourselves or to one another.
- If we can trust the wounds of a friend, surely we can trust the wounds that God lovingly imparts to us through the painful circumstances of life.
- Jacob wrestled with an angel of God and was wounded so that he walked the rest of his life with a limp (Gen 32:22). This wound was precisely what Jacob needed to remind him to trust in God and not in his own cleverness. It was a lesson he never fully mastered.

- Praise God for the hard side of his love. He is willing to use pain and suffering as tools to purge our sin and to mold us into the likeness of Jesus.

Wrath

The wrath of God is being revealed from heaven against all the godlessness and wickedness of men, who suppress the truth by their wickedness, since what may be known about God is plain to them, because God has made it plain to them.

—Rom 1:18–19

- A person who never gets angry is a monster. If, when evil and wicked things are done to people (the sexual abuse or exploitation of children, for example), such deeds do not rouse us to anger, then they expose a sin in us.
- Similarly, there are things that God will not abide that anger him. Whenever these things—these sins—are committed, they always produce the same, appropriate response in the form of God's anger.
- A day of judgment is coming when God will dispense justice against all sinners and their sins. Followers and lovers of Christ will not experience the wrath of God because God's wrath against their sin fell on "Jesus, who rescues us from the coming wrath" (1 Thess 1:10b) as he hung on the cross. God's righteous wrath was diverted from us to the One on the cross.
- Praise God for Jesus, our Sin-bearer and our Wrath-bearer.
- Praise God too for his future righteous judgment, which is cause for rejoicing: "Let the heavens rejoice, let the earth be glad; let the sea resound, and all that is in it; let the fields be jubilant, and everything in them. Then all the trees of the forest will sing for joy; they will sing before the Lord, *for he comes, he comes to judge the earth.* He will judge the world in righteousness and the peoples in his truth" (Ps 96:11–13).

Yoke-giver

Come to me, all you who are weary and burdened, and I will give you rest. Take *my yoke* upon you and learn from me, for I am gentle and humble in heart, and you will find rest for your souls. For *my yoke* is easy and my burden is light.

—Matt 11:28–30

- A yoke is a bar or frame that is attached to the necks of two work animals (such as oxen) so they can pull a plow or a heavy load.
- When we come to Christ, we are placed in a yoke so that we might work for him. But we do not labor alone. We are yoked together with Jesus so that we benefit from his power as we pull the plow in his field.
- Praise God for his easy yoke. Praise him too for his willingness to bind himself to us so that we can advance God's kingdom work on earth as a team.

*Glory be to the Father and to the Son and to the Holy Spirit.
As it was in the beginning, is now and forever shall be, world without end.
Amen.*

www.ingramcontent.com/pod-product-compliance
Lightning Source LLC
Chambersburg PA
CBHW061428300426
44114CB00014B/1582